Gender Analysis in Development Planning

Kumarian Press Library of Management for Development
Selected Titles

*Working Together: Gender Analysis in
Agriculture, Vols. 1 and 2*
edited by Hilary Sims Feldstein and
Susan V. Poats

*Gender Roles in Development Projects:
A Case Book,* edited by Catherine
Overholt, Mary B. Anderson, Kathleen
Cloud, and James E. Austin

*Getting to the 21st Century:
Voluntary Action and the Global Agenda*
David C. Korten

Training for Development, 2d Edition
Rolf P. Lynton and Udai Pareek

*Seeking Solutions: Framework and Cases for
Small Enterprise Development Programs*
Charles K. Mann, Merilee S. Grindle,
and Parker Shipton

*Opening the Marketplace to Small
Enterprise: Where Magic Ends
and Development Begins*
Ton de Wilde and Stijntje Schreurs,
with Arleen Richman

*Women's Ventures: Assistance to the
Informal Sector in Latin America*
edited by Marguerite Berger
and Mayra Buvinic

*The Family Planning Manager's Handbook:
Basic Skills and Tools for Managing
Family Planning Programs*
James A. Wolff, Linda J. Suttenfield,
and Susanna C. Binzen

*Democratizing Development:
The Role of Voluntary Organizations*
John Clark

Change in an African Village: Kefa Speaks
Else Skjønsberg

*Keepers of the Forest: Land Management
Alternatives in Southeast Asia*
edited by Mark Poffenberger

*The Water Sellers: A Cooperative
Venture of the Rural Poor*
Geoffrey D. Wood and Richard
Palmer-Jones, with M. A. S. Mandal,
Q. F. Ahmed, and S. C. Dutta

Gender Analysis in Development Planning

A Case Book

editors
Aruna Rao
Mary B. Anderson
Catherine A. Overholt

KUMARIAN PRESS

Gender Analysis in Development Planning: A Case Book.
Copyright © 1991 Kumarian Press, Inc. All rights reserved. No part of this book
may be reproduced or transmitted in any form or by any means, electronic or
mechanical, including photocopy, recording, or information storage and retrieval
system, without prior written permission of Kumarian Press, 630 Oakwood
Avenue, Suite 119, West Hartford, Connecticut 06110-1529 USA.

Printed in the United States of America
First edition published 1991

Cover design by Laura Augustine
Edited by Ida May Norton
Proofread by Kevin R. Frazzini
Typeset by Rosanne Pignone

Printed on acid-free paper by McNaughton & Gunn

Library of Congress Cataloging-in-Publication Data

Gender analysis in development planning : a case book / editors, Aruna Rao,
    Mary B. Anderson, Catherine A. Overholt
        p.   cm. — (Kumarian Press library of management for
    development)
    Includes bibliographical references.
    ISBN 0-931816-61-0 (alk. paper). — ISBN 0-931816-62-9 (teaching notes :
    alk. paper)
    1. Women in rural development—Developing countries—Case studies.
    2. Rural development projects—Developing countries—Case studies.
    I. Rao, Aruna. II. Anderson, Mary B., 1939–   . III. Overholt, Catherine,
    1942–   . IV. Series.
    HQ1240.5.D44G45   1991
    307.1′412′091724—dc20   91-31013

---

95   94   93   92   91   5   4   3   2   1

Contents

Figures

Introduction

Aruna Rao

ASIA IS CHARACTERIZED BY some of the world's starkest gender inequalities. In South Asia, these are most obvious in relation to the physical quality of life. Although statistics from around the world indicate that women in general live longer than men, the reverse is true for South Asia. In Europe and North America, where access to health facilities is the same for women and men, there are 5 percent more women in the population than men. In South Asia, there are 94 women to 100 men, that is, a deficit of 11 percent in comparison with the West (Sen 1989). Pakistan has the lowest average ratio of females to males in the population (90:100), but the lowest absolute ratio (84:100) is found in the Indian states of Punjab and Haryana, the prosperous Green Revolution states (Sen 1989). In South Asia (except Sri Lanka), female infant mortality rates exceed that of males. Also in South Asia (except Sri Lanka), the female illiteracy rate (66.3 percent) exceeds that of males by 20 percent (ESCAP 1989).

In Southeast and East Asia, which is characterized by some of the world's fastest growing economies, women, on average, enjoy decent living standards. Yet they face, as do their counterparts in South Asia, discrimination in employment, wages, and social status. In Thailand, for example, which is considered a newly industrializing country (NIC), with near-parity rates in male and female labor force participation and an 82.7 percent female literacy rate, 74 percent of women employed in 1980 were found in the agricultural sector. Of those, almost seven out of ten were unpaid family workers (Tonguthai 1987). Even if women are not concentrated in the marginal ranks of the labor force, they still face inequalities. Data on wage differentials for the region as a whole show that women consistently receive lower wages than their male counterparts. In the nonagricultural sector of most Asia-Pacific countries, there is not a large difference in the hours worked by women and men: on average, women work 90 hours to every 100 hours worked by men (ESCAP 1987, 24). In some countries, women work longer hours for lower pay. In Japan, for example, female manufacturing industry workers work slightly longer than their male counterparts, yet they earn only 45 to 55 percent of male wages (ESCAP 1987, 24). Only in some countries, such as the Philippines and the Republic of Korea, do wage differentials decline with increased levels of education (ESCAP 1987, 29).

Also, higher living standards in Southeast and East Asia do not go hand in hand with social equality. According to one recent international survey, social, political, and legal equality between men and women in Southeast and East Asia ranked above the high-growth economies of the Middle East but far below the developing economies of Latin America. Moreover, the difference in male/female levels of equality between South and Southeast Asia was minimal (Population Crisis Committee 1988). In fact, in that survey, Sri Lanka and India ranked far higher on women's social equality than did most Southeast Asian countries, including Thailand, Indonesia, Singapore, and Malaysia.

There is now undisputed evidence that the processes of growth and technological change make life better for some—but worse for the many who do not have the political influence to "secure pre-emptory measures or quick amelioration" (Bardhan 1987, 2). Until recently, discussions on poverty and on the employment effects of growth dealt only with aggregate terms and assumed that development processes and policies were gender-neutral in their impact:

> The employment effects of technological change, for example, were discussed mostly in terms of total labor input figures, without going on to ask if those displaced and those employed with . . . the new technology would be the same people, of the same gender, of the same class background, even if the net effect on the aggregate turned out to be positive or neutral (Bardhan 1987).

Most development policies and projects have in fact had severe negative impacts on the survival chances of poor women and their families. Moreover, such policies and large-scale projects often fail to meet their goals when women's labor contributions at the household and project levels are overlooked, their need for economic incentives are not understood, and resources relevant to their productive work are misdirected to men (Rao 1986).

But even in the face of such evidence, governments in Asia have not realigned development policies or altered the design of major economic projects in such a way as to support women's productive work and thus strengthen their contribution to national productivity goals. Major economic sectoral policies and resource allocations (which account for about 40 percent of total annual public expenditures in Asian countries) continue to be gender-blind (ESCAP 1989). As witnessed by the priority accorded women in national development plans, governments in Asia still view women as an adjunct to the main business of economic development and regard women in development (WID) issues as essentially a welfare concern. No Asian government explicitly has accorded women equality with men in the allocation of public resources or in the targeting of investments, although in this respect, governments in Asia are not unique (United Nations International Research and Training Institute for the Advancement of Women, INSTRAW n.d.). Women's concerns are treated explicitly only in the family planning, nutrition, and health sections of national development plans.

Further, the commonly pursued path of economic development primarily follows the profit motive, with development taking place in a socioeconomic context characterized by hierarchies and inequality. This approach has hurt the poor badly, and as Raj Krishna pointed out, "a development policy that hurts the poor will inevitably hurt poor women even more" (Krishna 1983, 10). Particularly in South Asia, "as development forces bring more and more of national resources like land, forests or water into the pale of the markets, [women's] extended domestic work for adding to the real incomes of families becomes increasingly more arduous" (Banerjee 1989, 5). Many poor households are de facto female-headed and supported primarily by women's meager earnings. But poor women find it increasingly difficult to make up the gap between poverty and survival.

Governments, particularly in South Asia (except Sri Lanka), simply have not allocated sufficient public resources to reduce women's extended domestic burden by provisioning poor families with basic minimum needs: guaranteed employment at least at a poverty-line income, health services, water and sanitation facilities, appropriate technologies to reduce the drudgery of women's home production activities, nurseries and day-care centers, and compulsory primary education. In South Asia, on average, education accounts for 6.7 percent of public expenditure (Southeast Asia spends twice that), and health accounts for approximately 3 percent throughout Asia (ESCAP 1989). In contrast, economic services (transportation and communications infrastructure and power) account for 35.5 percent of public expenditure in South Asia (ESCAP 1989). Moreover, research conducted at the end of the 1970s showed that the *minimum needs strategy* was not unaffordably expensive (ESCAP 1979). Basic needs at a minimum level could have been provided to all low-income communities in Asian countries had governments raised their social service outlay to at least 20 percent of total public expenditure and raised the proportion to at least 33 percent as income grew over the next decade (ESCAP 1979).

The evidence from around the world indicates that the provision of minimum needs does not need to wait for sustained high levels of economic growth. In fact, economic growth (though necessary in the long run) does not appear to be a sufficient condition for improvement in living standards. As an illustration, between 1960 and 1980, the countries that achieved the greatest reduction in their mortality rate for children under age five included low-growth countries such as Sri Lanka, Costa Rica, and Cuba, but did not include a number of high-growth countries such as Brazil (Sen 1989). Clearly, improvements in living standards require a rapid expansion in public resources allocated to social sectors: education, health, nutrition, and water and sanitation. In some countries, this wide distribution of resources has come before increased economic growth and in others after it (Sen 1989). The lesson seems to be that the fruits of development must be consciously distributed for specific purposes to specific populations—they do not simply trickle down.

Fairer distribution of the gains from development is central to the concept of integrating gender issues in development planning (Krishna 1983). Such a distribution, though motivated by equity considerations, nonetheless has long-term productivity consequences. The relationship between access to basic social services and female labor force participation is a case in point. Across the Asia region, it has been documented that the "female [labor force] participation rate is inversely related to household income per capita, especially in the lower ranges of income" (Krishna 1983, 4). In other words, poor women are under greater pressure to work for wages, however low, than are women from middle-income households, who also have better access to labor-saving household technologies. Poor women's work is essential to the survival of their families, but it often comes at the expense of their daughters' education and future income-earning opportunities. Extensive coverage of minimum needs might not only improve girls' educational prospects, but also might allow poor women to move out of the secondary or unorganized labor market (with its low wages, irregular and insecure jobs, and few worker benefits) and into the organized sector for a longer-term commitment.

But development planning as an instrument of distributive justice cannot stop at the doorstep of the household—it must step in. Various theories on the economic behavior of the household have assumed incorrectly that household allocational decisions proceed on the basis of a unitary utility function and maximize the rational allocation of resources toward the achievement of commonly held goals. In fact, it is becoming increasingly evident that "just as men and women differ in their participation in labor markets, in their wage rates, and in their prospects when marriages dissolve through death or separation, men and women also frequently differ with respect to allocational priorities" (Bruce and Dwyer 1988, 2). Gender inequalities in access to and control over resources in the world of income relations would suggest that a common ground plan is unlikely to serve men's and women's distinct self-interests within the family (Bruce and Dwyer 1988). In contrast to the earlier view of households as homogenous units, Sen characterizes households as bargaining units of "cooperative conflict." According to Sen's view, individuals within households primarily contend to gain their own ends, but their utilities (which in a poverty context relate primarily to survival needs rather than utilities such as "satisfaction" and so on) may overlap in many areas (Sen 1985).

What are the differences in the way men and women spend their income, and how do these affect family survival? A growing body of research indicates that women spend all or a greater portion of their income than do men on subsistence and nutrition. While gender-differentiated allocational priorities and responsibilities are most evident in Africa, such differences are not uncommon in Asia. For example, Kumar's study in Kerala, India, showed that a child's nutritional level increased proportionally with increases in the mother's income, food inputs from subsistence farming, and the quality of available family-based child care (Kumar 1977). Children's nutritional levels, however, did not increase in direct proportion to increases in parental income. Thus, what do gender-based allocational differences mean for development policy? The answer is simply that "individuals rather than households should be the recipients of economic outlays, whether transfers or wage earning opportunities, with women being more appropriate recipients when certain ends are desired" (Bruce and Dwyer 1988, 18).

The instruments available for transforming the political economy that conditions the status of women in society are many. Most important is the organized political power of women themselves. Women's organizations, particularly in South Asia, such as the Self-Employed Women's Association (SEWA) and the Working Women's Forum (WWF), have been effective not only in improving the material conditions of women. They also provide a sheltered space where women can explore different self-perceptions and foster a much-needed extrafamilial association through which women can interact with other women from their broader community. The starting point for women's advancement may lie within the household, but the key to changing household dynamics that discriminate against women (what Jain calls the "tyranny of the household") is the strength women gain (to confront oppressive conditions) from association and support from groups outside the family (Jain 1985). Although typically these women's groups are small, they represent women's voices and provide laboratories for experimentation and the engineering of social change. In the long run, this kind of group action can counteract the political weakness of individual women and raise their influence vis-à-vis other groups in the political arena as well (Corner 1986, 22).

Still, it is often the case that experiments that work well on a small scale do not lend themselves to large-scale operation because of "diseconomies of scale"—organizational, political, and economic (Tendler 1987). The fact remains that governments exert a powerful impact (both positive and negative) on poverty either directly through income distribution or indirectly through policies, for example, regarding agricultural development, credit subsidization, and tariff protection (Tendler 1987). This has impelled the concern to integrate gender into development planning. Indeed, public policy can also influence the role of markets and market imperfections in determining the allocation and reward for labor (a third instrument for transforming the conditions that determine the status of women in society).

Although the issue of integrating gender into development planning is essentially political in nature, at least some of the persistent gender-blindness in policy and programming can be traced to uncertainty over how the concept translates into appropriate and workable analytical tools. Thus, what are the ways of convincing development planners to take women into account? This key question has elicited a number of responses. One response has been to make visible women's "invisibility" in national income accounts by redefining "productive work" to include household production, to recount women's labor force participation, and to make monetary estimates of women's total contribution to national income. Another approach has focused on evaluating the gender-differentiated impact of mainstream economic development programs and sectoral policies.

In the early years of this decade, there were few studies of this kind. From 1984 to 1989, I coordinated a program for the Population Council in Asia on Women's Roles and Gender Differences in Development. The program covered five countries: India, Bangladesh, Thailand, Indonesia, and the Philippines. It aimed to strengthen planners' and practitioners' ability to generate and use information about women's social and economic roles in the design, implementation, and evaluation of large-scale projects and sectoral plans. Two major strategies were adopted in pursuance of this goal:

1. The production of case studies that (a) document the impact of gender-differentiated access to and control of valued resources (including labor and income) on the objectives of programs and on the lives and welfare of women and their families; and (b) suggest alternative planning and evaluation frameworks and management strategies that are sensitive to the gender factor in development.
2. Collaboration with (a) development training institutes in integrating materials on women's roles into programs geared toward development planners and practitioners within key sectors; and (b) planners and project personnel in working toward policy and program changes more beneficial to low-income women as well as men.

The Population Council program generated a total of eight studies on such issues as nonfarm rural employment, small-scale industries, and irrigation. Five of the studies have been published, and all have been widely distributed in Asia and elsewhere. Also, these materials have been discussed by the planners and program personnel directly involved in the program studied. In some cases, the authorities involved adopted the program design changes or policy recommendations highlighted in a study, which resulted in a more gender-equitable distribution of resources, promoted women's participation, and enhanced their labor productivity.

Finally, these studies, in their original format, have been used in short- and long-term training exercises and in academic courses around the world. For the purposes of teaching, five of the Asia studies have been reformatted into four case studies and are included in this publication. Teaching notes for all the cases have also been prepared and are available on request from Kumarian Press. The remaining two cases published here are drawn from studies I conducted in Asia between 1985 and 1988.

This case book is meant primarily for national development planners and practitioners as well as for staff of international development agencies. Those who are looking for a set of conceptual perspectives and analytical techniques to deal explicitly and effectively with gender issues in a range of development projects can use these cases as a pedagogical tool. Those who are new to gender issues will find that the cases present factual descriptions of actual projects that encourage application of the Gender Analysis Framework designed by Overholt et al. (1985), reproduced in the next section of this book, and allow for thinking purposefully about issues that are highly relevant to their professional work. The analytical framework is, in essence, a means of making visible what women do and why. It is a process of building a gender-differentiated data base on activities, access to resources, and control over resources, and on factors influencing these three issues, in a way that facilitates translation into project or policy terms.

Because the cases in this volume have been reformatted for teaching by the case method approach, they contain no analysis. Rather, "they provide the raw material from which the participants can engage in their own analysis and draw their own conclusions" (Overholt et al. 1985, xiii). The cases do not discuss theories or hypotheses. As in the real world, they do not have a "right answer," but offer many reasonable alternatives and defensible recommendations (Overholt et al. 1985, xiii). Because the case method approach to training is grounded in the philosophy that participants must take an active part in and share the responsibility for the learning process, problem-solving skills are developed in the process of systematically deriving a logical and sensible set of conclusions (Overholt et al. 1985). Using these cases in particular, development personnel can increase their knowledge and skills to address issues related to the role of women in development at the project and policy levels. This should enhance opportunities for women's contribution to development and facilitate their access to the benefits of development. If this in turn helps poor women lead the life they want to lead, then development planning can do no better.

Gender Analysis Framework

Catherine A. Overholt, Kathleen Cloud,
Mary B. Anderson, and James E. Austin

(Formerly "Women in Development: A Framework for Project Analysis," chapter in Overholt et al., *Gender Roles in Development Projects: Cases for Planners* [Kumarian Press, 1985].)

DEVELOPMENT PLANNING HAS FAILED to recognize fully or systematically women's contribution to the development process or, in turn, the effect of this process on them. This failure has limited development efforts and effects. Economic growth, project efficiency, and social justice call for a new approach to development that systematically includes women.

In her seminal work of 1970, Ester Boserup plainly articulated the state of neglect: "In the vast and ever-growing literature on economic development, reflections on the particular problems of women are few and far between."[1] Over the last decade, the issues regarding the integral involvement of women in national development processes have slowly crept onto the agendas of national and international development agencies. By 1980, many countries and international agencies had explicitly incorporated women's issues into their development plans and had set up special bureaus, offices, or even ministries as the organizational focal point of these new concerns. Furthermore, the barren literature fields observed by Boserup had begun to produce intellectual harvests. By 1981, articles and books in the women in development area were appearing at a rapid rate.

Although there has been much activity, development planning efforts still fail to recognize fully women's actual and potential contribution to the development process or the effect of the development process on them.

The imperatives for rectifying these inadequacies are based on both economic and equity concerns. Women are key actors in the economic system, yet their neglect in development plans has left untapped a potentially large economic contribution. Women represent the majority of the population, but they are concentrated at the bottom of the ladder in terms of employment, education, income, and status. Both economic growth and social justice call for increased attention to the integration of women into the development process. This paper proceeds from the basis that equity and economic growth are compatible objectives and must be pursued simultaneously.

Projects are among the primary vehicles used by governments and international agencies to channel resources in the development process.[2] One of the barriers[3] to translating research activity about women into effective and beneficial development programming has been the absence of an adequate analytical framework for integrating women into project analysis. Such integration of women is essential for transforming policy concerns into practical realities.[4] The purpose of this paper is to present an analytical framework that will facilitate this process.

Analytical Framework

What women do will have an impact on most projects whether or not women are considered explicitly in their design and implementation. Similarly, most projects will have an effect on women's lives. The framework we propose can improve the definition of general project objectives, assess how these relate to women's involvement with a project, and anticipate the effect of the project on women. The analysis we introduce here is not intended to be limited in its application to projects directed only to women. This analysis is equally applicable, and probably more important, precisely for projects where women's roles and responsibilities have not been explicitly noted but are implicitly assumed in project design and implementation.

Development projects are vehicles for generating change. Project design and implementation, therefore, require an adequate data base. "Visibility" is the starting point for integrating women into development projects and visibility also comes through data. Thus, the cornerstone of the proposed framework is an adequate data base that considers what women do and why. The key challenge, however, is how to organize and present this information so as to facilitate its translation into project terms. The framework we propose uses four interrelated components: activity profile; access and control profile; analysis of factors influencing activities, access, and control; and project cycle analysis.

The first component, the *activity profile*, is based on the concept of a gender-based division of labor. The activity profile will delineate the economic activities of the population in the project area first by age and gender and then by ethnicity, social class, or other important distinguishing characteristics. In addition, it will indicate the amount of time spent by individuals to accomplish these activities. The second component, the *access and control profile,* will identify what resources individuals can command to carry out their activities and the benefits they derive from them.

Analysis of factors influencing activities, access, and control focuses on the underlying factors that determine the gender division of labor and gender-related control over resources and benefits. These analyses identify the factors that create differential opportunities or constraints for men's and women's participation in and benefits from projects. Because the work that men and women carry out shifts over time in response to the processes of change, an understanding of the underlying trends within the broader economic and cultural environment must be incorporated into this analysis.

The final component of the analytic framework, *project cycle analysis,* consists of examining a project in light of the foregoing basic data and the trends that are likely to affect it and/or be generated by it. Together, these four components provide a sufficient basis for designing and implementing projects that can best benefit women and benefit by women's participation.

Activity Profile

To assess the interaction between women and projects, it is important to know what women do. How one categorizes activities conceptually is important. We suggest the following categories:

Production of Goods and Services

Too often planners have failed to recognize women's roles as producers. Specific productive activities carried out for all goods and services by men or women should be identified. It is not sufficient to identify only female activities. Male activities must also be specified, because the interrelationships can affect or be affected by the project.

Since general topologies can be very misleading, specific delineation of activities is needed for each country and project setting. Huntington's critique of the early Boserup work emphasized the difficulties of generalizing: "[E]ven if the classification and causal relationships of Boserup's conceptualization are pertinent to African societies, they do not hold elsewhere."[5] The work of Deere and Leon in Andean areas reinforces the problem with generalization: "Boserup's propositions . . . hold only for the middle and rich states of the peasantry. . . ."[6]

The degree of specificity of the activity listing should depend on the nature of the project. Those areas most directly associated with a project should carry the greatest detail. For example, if the project concerns a new agricultural production technology, then the gender division of labor for each agricultural productive activity should be delineated, e.g., land clearance, preparation, seeding, weeding, and processing.

Reproduction and Maintenance of Human Resources

Activities that are carried out to produce and care for the family members need to be specified according to who does them. They might include but are not limited to fuel and water collection, food preparation, birthing, child care, education, health care, and laundry. These activities are often viewed as noneconomic, generally carry no pecuniary remuneration, and usually are excluded from the national income accounts. In fact, these household maintenance tasks are essential economic functions that ensure the development and preservation of the human capital for the family and the nation. Galbraith observed that "what is not counted is usually not noticed."[7] In project analyses, not noticing a major activity can lead to defective project design.

Giving explicit attention to these functions is critical. Women's project involvement can depend on whether or how a project affects reproduction and maintenance activities, the production of goods and services, and/or the interrelationship between these activities. The scarcest resource for most low-income women is time. The design of projects that increase time requirements for particular activities must consider these requirements in relation to the time required for other necessary activities.

The activities listed in the above categories need to be further classified to increase their utility for the subsequent project analysis. Three parameters are suggested for describing the activities:

1. Gender and age denomination—identifies whether women, men, their children, or the elderly carry out an activity; reveals gender patterns in the work activities; and is the key to identifying subsequent gender effects.
2. Time allocation—specifies what percentage of time is allocated to each activity and whether it is seasonal or daily.
3. Activity locus—specifies where the activity is being performed (in the home, in the family field or shop, or in the outside community); reveals female mobility; and carries implications for project delivery systems.

Table A provides an example of how information on activities can be summarized.

Most projects are not targeted to homogeneous population groups. The gender-based division of labor as well as the access to and control over resources and benefits are likely to differ, often quite substantially, according to socioeconomic class or ethnic affiliation. Therefore, it is essential to develop the activity profiles separately for each of the distinct population groups to whom the project is targeted.

Access and Control Profile

Identifying the gender-specific activities in production, reproduction, and maintenance is a necessary, but not sufficient, step in the data preparation for project design and implementation. The flow of resources and benefits is a fundamental concept in the analysis of how projects will affect and be affected by women. Of particular concern is the access that individuals have to resources for carrying out their activities and the command they have over the benefits that derive from these activities. Table B illustrates how this information can be usefully summarized.

Two points are important here. First, it is essential to differentiate between access and control. Access to resources does not necessarily imply the power to control them. To control a situation is to impose one's own definition upon the other actors in that situation.[8] In other words, access can be determined by others, but control implies that one is the determining force.

Second, it is also important to differentiate between access and control over the use of resources, on the one hand, and access to and control over the benefits derived from the mobilization of resources. Even where women have unrestrained use of resources, they are not always able to realize the gains from their use. Huntington's observation on female-dominated African agriculture illustrates this situation. Men have power and control over the fruits of women's labor because "tradition gives men a position of authority over women. . . . Men get their wealth, their livelihood and their leisure from women's labor."[9] By focusing on both resources and benefits, one obtains an accurate assessment of the relative power of members of a society or economy and can utilize this knowledge to analyze the probable interaction of women with a project and its likely effect on them.

Analysis of Factors Influencing Activities, Access, and Control

The factors that determine who does what in any population subgroup and what access and control individuals will have to resources and benefits are broad and interrelated. They could be categorized in numerous ways. We suggest the following:

1. General economic conditions, such as poverty levels, inflation rates, income distribution, international terms of trade, infrastructure;
2. Institutional structures, including the nature of government bureau-

cracies and arrangement for the generation and dissemination of knowledge, technology, and skills;
3. Demographic factors;
4. Sociocultural factors;
5. Community norms, such as familial norms and religious beliefs;
6. Legal parameters;
7. Training and education;
8. Political events, both internal and external.

The reason for specifying these determining factors is to identify which can facilitate or constrain a project. Some factors, if not most, will not be amenable to change by a project. Therefore, the task for project design and implementation is to assess the above factors in terms of whether and how they will have an effect on or be affected by a project.

In addition, it is important to identify the exogenous trends or dynamic forces that are already affecting change on what men and women actually do. Projects are not implemented and carried out within the static environment implied by the activity and access and control profiles. Dynamic forces—political, social, environmental, or physical—can either enhance the accomplishment of a project's objectives or seriously impede it.

The consideration of exogenous trends and dynamic forces, while always important, is even more so in relation to women. There are a number of forces affecting women on a worldwide basis. Life expectancy is rising, particularly for women. Availability of birth control information and techniques combined with declining infant mortality rates have the potential to change a fundamental determinant of women's activities; women may have fewer births and/or raise the same number or fewer children. Women are taking up productive activities previously undertaken by men as men migrate to cities or as women assume responsibilities as heads of their households. Women are increasingly entering wage labor occupations in order to survive or to maintain a standard of living. Women are gaining increasing access to permanent wage labor in some areas.

In many areas, the number of women-headed households is increasing, although there tends to be a cultural lag in acknowledging this fact. Bangladesh provides an important case in point. The number of women who were left destitute, widowed, or abandoned after the war has had a significant effect on the Bangladesh cultural norm that all women should be under the care and protection of a man. Decreasing land availability is also challenging the norm that children are an asset. Children now cannot be absorbed onto family land, but must be educated in order to earn a living. Costs of education raise the costs of childrearing significantly. Decreasing land/human ratios also mean that it is more difficult for a man to support all the dependent female family members. The trend is toward an abdication of this traditional responsibility. While these forces have direct and important effects on women's lives and the activities they perform, they are part of a much larger dynamic process. The status of women and their involvement in work external to the household is changing in Bangladesh without anyone's having designed this process. Project design and implementation for Bangladesh must take these forces into account in order to understand the context in which a project will be working and the forces that will affect it.

While Bangladesh provides an example of broader national trends that influence projects, there are also a number of international trends that affect local circumstances. Worldwide inflation, international transfers of labor, the impact of technologies, international tensions including the Cold War, all change over time and can affect project outcomes. Events within a project may be better understood when these larger forces are explicitly noted and considered in project planning, implementation, and evaluation.

Project Cycle Analysis

The remainder of the analytical framework consists of examining a project in light of the foregoing basic data. The process is to ask which activities the project will affect and how the issues of access and control relate to these activities. The factors that determine who undertakes particular activities and with what access and control are critical because they act as mediators for the project's effects on women. The analysis will help pinpoint areas of a project that have to be adjusted in order to achieve the desired outcome.

At the project identification stage, questions that relate to women as project clientele need to be addressed. This includes defining project objectives in terms of women, identifying the opportunities and/or constraints for women's project involvement, and, finally, identifying possible negative effects on women. In the design stage of the project, questions related to the impact on women's activities and access and control of resources and benefits need to be raised. For project implementation, questions regarding the relationship of women in the project area to project personnel, organizational structures, operations, logistics, and so on need to be considered. Finally, data requirements for evaluating the project's effects on women must be addressed. Specific questions related to project cycle analysis are detailed in Table C.

The activity analysis and the access and control analysis applied to the project cycle analysis provide the basis for good project development. They guide project identification by revealing where women are and what they are doing. They assist project design by highlighting the problem areas and their causes. The challenge is to find ways to deal with the problem areas either by removing them, bypassing them, or adjusting project expectations within them. Project implementation has to be considered in the design process and can benefit from the analytical data, too. It is important to recognize that no standard project design is possible. Each country's situation is unique and will require specific responses.

Cross-Cultural Uses of the Analytical Framework

The analytical framework we have provided here is a useful device for understanding the roles of men and women in a society and the external forces that may affect project planning. The analysis is generalizable in every context in that it is relevant to determine the gender-based division of labor and to understand the forces that act as constraints on this division or that act to change it.

In applying any generalized analysis across projects and across cultures, it is important to bear in mind its precise use and its clear limits. When activity analysis shows that women are involved in certain productive tasks in one area and that these tasks have certain implications for the division of resources and of power in that context, it is unlikely that even this same division of labor will have exactly the same implications for the division of power in any other culture or project location. Traditions, customs, and political processes interact with economic and social activities differently in different settings. Transference of conclusions and interpretations across projects and cultures is unlikely to be accurate. Nonetheless, there may be similarities in the mode of analysis that may be applied to understand these interactions. While the analytical framework suggested here raises questions that are applicable in all settings insofar as it is designed to gather critically relevant information for project design, one must apply it to specific project settings. Good project design requires actual data on what work women do and in what context, together with clear specification of the issues of prestige, power, access, and control.

A decade has passed since the Percy Amendment required that U.S. bilateral assistance programs

> be administered so as to give particular attention to those programs, projects and activities which tend to integrate women into the national economies of foreign countries, thus improving their status and assisting the total development effort.[10]

This legislative mandate requires that women be cast as contributors and agents of economic development as well as its beneficiaries. Planners, therefore, must guard against the negative effects of their projects on women and focus on the need to enhance women's productivity, raise their income, and promote their access to economically productive resources as a means to achieving overall national economic growth.

Conclusion

The foregoing framework should be viewed as a flexible instrument rather than a rigid format for accomplishing this objective. It does not pretend to be a definitive work, but rather one upon which others can build. Only in that spirit can we continue to learn together, and that collective process is essential to the progress we pursue.

Table A Activity Profile

Socioeconomic Activity	FA	MA	FC	MC	FE	ME	Time[2]	Locus[3]
1. Production of Goods and Services								
a. Product/Services								
1. Functional Activity								
2. Functional Activity								
3. Functional Activity								
b. Product/Services								
1. Functional Activity								
2. Functional Activity								
3. Functional Activity								
2. Reproduction and Maintenance of Human Resources								
a. Product/Services								
1. Functional Activity								
2. Functional Activity								
3. Functional Activity								
b. Product/Services								
1. Functional Activity								
2. Functional Activity								
3. Functional Activity								
1. Functional Activity								
1. Functional Activity								

Header spanning Gender/Age[1]

[1] FA = Female Adult; MA = Male Adult; FC = Female Child; MC = Male Child; FE = Female Elder; ME = Male Elder
[2] Percentage of time allocated to each activity; seasonal; daily
[3] Within home; family, field or shop; local community; beyond community

Table B Access and Control Profile

Resources	Access (M/F)	Control (M/F)
Land		
Equipment		
Labor		
Production		
Reproduction		
Capital		
Education/Training		

Benefits	*Access* *(M/F)*	*Control* *(M/F)*
Outside Income		
Assets Ownership		
In-kind Goods		
(food, clothing, shelter, etc.)		
Education		
Political Power/Prestige		
Other		

Table C   Key Questions for Project Cycle Analysis

WOMEN'S DIMENSION IN PROJECT IDENTIFICATION

A. Assessing Women's Needs
1. What needs and opportunities exist for increasing women's productivity and/or production?
2. What needs and opportunities exist for increasing women's access to and control of resources?
3. What needs and opportunities exist for increasing women's access to and control of benefits?
4. How do these needs and opportunities relate to the country's other general and sectoral development needs and opportunities?
5. Have women been directly consulted in identifying such needs and opportunities?

B. Defining General Project Objectives
1. Are project objectives explicitly related to women's needs?
2. Do these objectives adequately reflect women's needs?
3. Have women participated in setting those objectives?
4. Have there been any earlier efforts?
5. How has present proposal built on earlier activity?

C. Identifying Possible Negative Effects
1. Might the project reduce women's access to or control of resources and benefits?
2. Might it adversely affect women's situation in some other way?
3. What will be the effects on women in the short and longer run?

WOMEN'S DIMENSION IN PROJECT DESIGN

A. Project Impact on Women's Activities
1. Which of these activities (production, reproduction & maintenance, socio-political) does the project affect?
2. Is the planned component consistent with the current gender denomination for the activity?
3. If it plans to change the women's performance of that activity (i.e., locus of activity, remunerative mode, technology, mode of activity), is this feasible, and what positive or negative effects would it have on women?
4. If it does not change it, is this a missed opportunity for women's roles in the development process?

5. How can the project design be adjusted to increase the above-mentioned positive effects, and reduce or eliminate the negative ones?

B. Project Impact on Women's Access and Control
1. How will each of the project components affect women's access to and control of the resources and benefits engaged in and stemming from the production of goods and services?
2. How will each of the project components affect women's access to and control of the resources and benefits engaged in and stemming from the reproduction and maintenance of the human resources?
3. How will each of the project components affect women's access to and control of the resources and benefits engaged in and stemming from the sociopolitical functions?
4. What forces have been set into motion to induce further exploration of constraints and possible improvements?
5. How can the project design be adjusted to increase women's access to and control of resources and benefits?

WOMEN'S DIMENSION IN PROJECT IMPLEMENTATION

A. Personnel
1. Are project personnel sufficiently aware of and sympathetic toward women's needs?
2. Are women used to deliver the goods or services to women beneficiaries?
3. Do personnel have the necessary skills to provide any special inputs required by women?
4. What training techniques will be used to develop delivery systems?
5. Are there appropriate opportunities for women to participate in project management positions?

B. Organizational Structures
1. Does the organizational form enhance women's access to resources?
2. Does the organization have adequate power to obtain resources needed by women from other organizations?
3. Does the organization have the institutional capability to support and protect women during the change process?

C. Operations and logistics
1. Are the organization's delivery channels accessible to women in terms of personnel, location, and timing?
2. Do control procedures exist to ensure dependable delivery of the goods and services?
3. Are there mechanisms to ensure that the project resources or benefits are not usurped by males?

D. Finances
1. Do funding mechanisms exist to ensure program continuity?
2. Are funding levels adequate for proposed tasks?
3. Is preferential access to resources by males avoided?
4. Is it possible to trace funds for women from allocation to delivery with a fair degree of accuracy?

E. Flexibility
1. Does the project have a management information system that will allow it to detect the effects of the operation on women?

2. Does the organization have enough flexibility to adapt its structures and operations to meet the changing or newfound situations of women?

WOMEN'S DIMENSION IN PROJECT EVALUATION

A. Data Requirements
1. Does the project's monitoring and evaluation system explicitly measure the project's effects on women?
2. Does it also collect data to update the Activity Analysis and the Women's Access and Control Analysis?
3. Are women involved in designating the data requirements?

B. Data Collection and Analysis
1. Are the data collected with sufficient frequency so that necessary project adjustments could be made during the project?
2. Are the data fed back to project personnel and beneficiaries in an understandable form and on a timely basis to allow project adjustments?
3. Are women involved in the collection and interpretation of data?
4. Are data analyzed so as to provide guidance to the design of other projects?
5. Are key areas for WID research identified?

Notes

1. Ester Boserup, *Women's Role in Economic Development* (London: George Allen and Unwin Ltd., 1970).

2. This focus on "projects" rather than processes, institutions, and policies can inhibit rather than promote development if not managed appropriately. See David C. Korten, "Community Organization and Rural Development: A Learning Process Approach," *Public Administration Review* 40 (1980), pp. 480–503. Our attention to projects does not carry a normative judgment on this approach but rather reflects a concern to improve the existing modalities.

3. The perceptions or biases of "planners" concerning women constitute another barrier. See Barbara Rogers, *The Domestication of Women: Discrimination in Developing Societies* (London: Tavistock Publications, 1980).

4. See Gloria Scott, *The Invisible Woman* (Washington, D.C.: World Bank, 1980).

5. Sue Ellen Huntington, "Issues in Women's Role in Economic Development: Critique and Alternatives," *Journal of Marriage and the Family* (November 1975), p. 104.

6. C. Deere and M. Leon de Leal, *Women in Andean Agriculture: Peasant Production and Rural Wage Employment in Columbia and Peru* (Geneva: ILO, 1982).

7. Kenneth Galbraith, "The Economics of the American Housewife," *Atlantic Monthly* (August 1973), p. 79.

8. Alan Dawe, "The Two Sociologies," *British Journal of Sociology* 21 (1970), p. 207; also cited in Rogers, *op. cit.*

9. Huntington, *op. cit.*

10. U.S. Congress Foreign Assistance Act of 1973, Sections 103–107.

Cases

Case 1

Bangladesh: The Chandpur Irrigation Project

> Morning. The sun has long risen but the dew lifts slowly.
> Concealed by wisps of clouds and the mist of rising dew,
> the sun sheds its light. A breeze comes, with it the scent
> of ripened rice. It is Kartik, early November, the lushest
> month for rice in the fields and the leanest month for
> people in the villages. The stocks of rice in their homes
> and the demand for their labor will remain low until
> harvest. . . . Land and water. Fields and riverways. Fields
> upon fields lift out of the mist and fade into the distance.
> Fields laced by pools of standing water or streams of flow-
> ing water. The standing water reflects the clouds over-
> head. The flowing water sparkles in the sunlight. Land is
> peace—the source of all well-being. Water is fickle—a
> source of both well-being and destruction.
> —M.A. Chen, *A Quiet Revolution*

MOST OF THE LAND mass in Bangladesh is river delta formed by the silting of the Rivers Ganges, Meghna, and Brahmaputra. This low-lying land is subject to a harsh cycle of severe flooding in the rainy season and drought in the dry season. Crops suffer from too much or too little water. The con-tinual calamities this cycle generates limit economic progress. To ease the problems of the flood and drought cycle, large-scale capital-intensive flood control and irrigation projects have been initiated in the area. The Chand-pur irrigation project is one of these.

Bangladesh is not a large country in land mass. With a total population of 107 million, its population density is second only to Singapore's. Eighty-

---

This case was adapted for teaching by Leslie W. Tuttle and Mary B. Anderson from Chowdhury, Karim, and Begum (1989); Islam (1988); and Thompson (1986).

four percent of the people live in more than 70,000 villages. Almost half of these households are landless or nearly landless. Half of those who do own land own less than one acre, an area insufficient to support a family's subsistence existence.

In recent decades, patterns of land ownership have shifted. Polarization has occurred. On the one hand, consolidation has meant that some people have increasingly large landholdings; on the other, fragmentation has resulted in a growing number of small holdings and increasing landlessness. In 1986, annual per capita GNP in Bangladesh was U.S. $160.

Another indicator of the poverty and hardship of living conditions in Bangladesh is female mortality. There are only five countries in the world where men live longer than women. One of these in Bangladesh. Life expectancy under the age of fifteen is lower for females than for males. After fifteen, longevity figures favor women.

Development of Chandpur Irrigation Project

The Chandpur irrigation project (CIP) originated in 1963 with funding from the International Development Association (IDA) and two World Bank credits. Construction was interrupted twice, first by the Indo-Pakistan war of 1965 and, second, by the liberation war of 1971. These upheavals significantly disrupted the project. The objectives of the project were (1) to protect and increase agricultural production, especially the production of food grains; (2) to increase agricultural employment; and (3) to improve the living conditions for the people within the project area.

The project involved both the construction of embankments and modern irrigation facilities and the introduction of improved agricultural practices using high-yielding varieties (HYV) of crops. Irrigation and HYV rice would increase crop productivity of farmers in the area. In addition, there were plans to organize landless people to take advantage of new fishing opportunities in the newly constructed canals.

Construction of the canal system was completed in 1977. Operations began the following year. In total, 348 miles of canals for irrigation and drainage were built in the project area. Almost 1,500 low-lift pumps were installed to facilitate irrigation.

The system serviced an area of 220 square miles along the east bank of the Meghna River, where a population of at least 700,000 people lived. A circular embankment, 63 miles long, was constructed to protect 132,000 acres of land, of which 72,000 were arable and used for agriculture. A pump house in the northern sector was built to regulate the flow of the Dakatia River for irrigation and flood control. A regulator in the southwest sector was installed to drain water out of the Dakatia River into the Meghna and to provide flood control.

The construction phase of the project was undertaken by the Bangladesh Water Development Board (BWDB). A BWDB project director was in charge of the system's operation. His staff included representatives of BWDB and several other government agencies involved in agricultural extension and rural development. Although the construction phase did not involve significant participation by the villagers, they were later organized into irrigation groups to facilitate the distribution and operation of pumps and the collection of user fees. The impact of both the irrigation and flood protection changed the lives of the villagers.

Cropping Patterns and Intensity

The introduction of irrigation and flood control in the project area allowed farmers to grow high-yielding varieties of rice paddy during both the summer and winter growing seasons.

Summer

Before the irrigation project, two summer paddy crops were sown in April by broadcasting the seed. These two varieties ripened at different times, and the double cropping safeguarded the farmers against total loss in the case of damage by flood or drought. The names of the paddy were derived from their seasons of harvest: *aus* for August and *amon* for November. Both types of rice were low-yielding varieties grown without irrigation. Jute, a cash crop and the nation's largest export product, was also double cropped with amon.

The Chandpur irrigation project changed cropping patterns, but it did not lessen cropping intensity. The summer double crops of aus and amon paddy and jute were replaced with high-yielding amon paddy that required transplanting. This amon paddy has become the most common paddy crop in Bangladesh.

Vegetables, used with the basic grain in most meals, were grown in Bangladesh throughout the year. However, summer crops frequently suffered from waterlogging in low-lying areas such as Chandpur. Before irrigation, vegetables were grown in the fields alongside other crops, but irrigation made this impossible. Thus, women began to cultivate vegetable gardens in their homesteads. Spice cultivation, mostly peppers, was also highly labor-intensive and carried out at home.

Winter

In preproject days, the winter crops in the CIP area included wheat, vegetables, spices, pulses, and oil seeds. Wheat was grown as a secondary staple food between December and April. However, even though national policies had attempted to increase wheat production, these had never been entirely successful because the growers recognized that most people preferred to eat rice. Thus, they had little interest in increasing wheat production when there was little demand for the crop.

Pulses were grown also on a limited basis. Because the seeds of pulses were broadcast on marshy land after flood water receded, no plowing was required. Urea was used for fertilizer. However, this traditional cultivation method produced a very low yield. Similarly, traditional oil seed cultivation produced a limited crop.

With the implementation of the CIP, winter cropping patterns changed. Boro paddy, a winter high-yielding variety that required four times as much water as wheat, replaced most traditional winter crops once irrigation was available through CIP.

People and Their Activities in the CIP Area

Land ownership, family composition, and gender were the key determinants of employment and work activities for the villagers in the CIP area. The households of the project could be classified into five groups on the basis of land ownership.

1. *The landless.* Men in this category worked primarily as agricultural laborers for wages. Women in this group were responsible for collecting fuel, tending kitchen gardens, fetching water, keeping the home and home compound, preparing food and washing dishes, laundering clothes, and caring for children. They also hired themselves out for seasonal agricultural labor or as household servants in the homes of wealthier neighbors.

2. *Tenants.* The tenant farmers were sharecroppers who provided their own inputs and cultivated the land belonging to a landlord. In return for using the land, they paid the landlord one-half of their agricultural production. The women from sharecropping homes were also responsible for all domestic tasks as well as performing all the postharvest operations required by their share of the crop. This involved threshing, husking, winnowing, and boiling paddy to produce rice either for home consumption or for sale. It was possible to sell processed rice for a much higher return than could be realized by selling paddy.

3. *Small landowners* (less than one acre). The small landowners worked their own land, but also needed other forms of employment to supplement their incomes. They worked most often as sharecroppers or agricultural laborers. The women in this group performed domestic tasks and handled postharvest operations. According to custom and the observance of purdah, they did not work outside their homes. Small landowning families generally looked for alternative nonagricultural occupations for some members of their families. Traditionally, the male head of the household and the eldest son(s) managed the farming. Younger sons were encour-

aged to find other types of employment, preferably in a service industry.

4. *Midsize landowners* (one to three acres). These farmers cultivated their own land and, during peak seasons, hired extra labor to help. Women did domestic production and postharvest operations and never worked outside their homes.

5. *Large landowners* (more than three acres). This class was considered wealthy in Chandpur. The men from this group generally did not engage in any physical labor. Rather, they acted as farm managers in supervisory roles. They were also the community leaders in village social, religious, and political activities. The official village-level political body was under their control. This was true despite an official reservation of council seats for a wider representation of the community and for women. Wives, daughters, and mothers of these landowners, like women of other households, were responsible for household activities and postharvest processing of the crops grown on their land.

All families in the CIP area regarded education as the means for gaining nonagricultural employment. Middle- and higher-income families sought to educate their sons in order to be able to send them out for other work, but children of the poorest families remained illiterate and looked forward to agricultural employment for their livelihoods.

Status for men in the CIP area villages was measured by their ability to avoid physical labor. The man who hired others to work on his farm, under his supervision, enjoyed the most prestige. For women, familial and community respect derived from the performance of domestic and postharvest-related tasks for their households.

Living Conditions in the CIP Area

High demand for male labor occurred during the transplanting, weeding, and harvesting seasons. Male agricultural laborers worked for wages averaging twenty-five takas a day. During other seasons, there was widespread unemployment and underemployment of male workers. Females from the poorest households also worked in agriculture during peak seasons and suffered seasonal unemployment. However, because they also were hired for postharvest activities, their employment season was longer than that for males. Women received one kilo of rice for an eight-hour day of agricultural labor. If they worked into the evening, they were compensated with an evening meal.

This payment was not insignificant. In the CIP area, the poorest families typically ate only two meals a day, and only one of those included rice. The rich ate three rice meals each day. The poorest could afford milk or eggs once a week, middle-income families ate them every few days, and the rich every day. Meat or fish appeared at the holidays for the poorest and once a month for most people in the area. As incomes increased, the frequency of having meat or fish rose to weekly and, finally, daily for the rich.

In all households, the head of household was given the best and choicest foods in the largest quantities. Children shared equally regardless of age or sex. Elder women were given extra food in deference to their age and status. Finally, the rest of the women shared what was left, and at times of food shortage, they often ate less than other family members. The allocation of food was managed by these women, who described this system as "the way it has always been done" and "exactly as it should be."

Cultural norms in the CIP area meant that men were considered dominant in their families, and women showed their respect by deferring on decisions to their husbands. Women sometimes expressed their views and their husbands listened to them, but on all matters of importance—such as buying and selling land, business, crop choices, marriages, moving and the education of children—men were responsible for final decisions. Women gave their shopping lists to their husbands to take to market because only very poor women appeared in the marketplace. Thus, cash expenditures were in men's hands. Women often, therefore, did not consider it their business to know the family's exact landholdings, income, or cash flow.

Village households consisted of *baris*, groups of houses occupied by related family members and functioning in a communal manner. Often these families shared a single kitchen. Sometimes individual families moved from sharing common living quarters and the kitchen shed to establishing houses of their own. However, the extended family and its physical grouping in the *bari* continued to be the predominant form of domestic life for most people of all classes in the CIP area.

Houses were constructed of a range of materials that reflected income: mud and straw for the poorest households, variations of jute, tin, and brick for families with more resources. In areas most subject to flooding, construction materials meant the difference between homes that stood and those that did not. Brick housing had the best survival record.

In addition to trying to generate a subsistence living from the land, village families also allocated some resources toward guaranteeing secure and comfortable futures for their children. Indirectly, in the case of sons, this also provided for the parents' security in their old age because boys were responsible for caring for their elderly mothers and fathers. Therefore, living conditions of the family in the present were partly dependent on how successful past investments had been and on the proportion of family resources currently invested toward future returns.

The investment for boys was in the form of education. Families that could afford to do so kept their sons in school through high school so that they could be eligible for nonfarm employment. For girls, apart from cosmetics and clothes needed for attracting husbands, the investment took the form of a dowry. The higher the offered dowry, the greater the chances of marrying into a secure and wealthier family. The costs of school fees and supplies, the opportunity costs of keeping children in school, and the savings required for daughters' dowries were major expenses in Chandpur, determining a family's well-being and future prospects.

Impact of the Chandpur Irrigation Project

Crop yields were significantly increased in the CIP area as a result of the introduction of irrigation and flood control (see Tables 1.1 and 1.2). The cultivation of broadcast aus and amon paddy and double cropping of amon and jute were discontinued by farmers. They moved entirely to transplanted amon paddy, in 1987 cultivating 93 percent of the total land with transplanted amon for the first time. The net return per acre was 57 percent higher than it had been with broadcast paddy and 54 percent higher than with the amon and jute crop combination. Irrigation also changed the winter cropping pattern, displacing wheat, pulses, oil seeds, vegetables, and spices with high-yielding boro paddy.

Villages just outside the irrigation area responded to the regional changes by adopting potatoes as a cash crop. They instituted some local irrigation methods, including ponds, ditches, and canals with low-lift pumps, and found they could get high net returns per acre. Breaking with tradition, women in those areas began to participate in the field cultivation of the potato and other vegetable crops because these had become in short supply in the irrigated areas of CIP and could be sold there.

As a result of the irrigation, large landowners required more hired labor, and the landless found more agricultural work. However, because landowning men were not fully employed before the irrigation, they could supply some of their own increased labor needs, and thus the demand for hired male labor for the cultivation of transplanted paddy was not proportionately as large as the increase in production. Therefore, even though more work for male agricultural laborers became available, a sharp increase in their wages did not occur.

In contrast, the increased demand for female labor in postharvest operations and as domestic help was very high. Women in landowning families could not compete for this work for two reasons. The first was purdah, which restricted all but the poorest women from working outside their *baris*. Second, because the increase in production yields generated more postharvest work for women in their own homes, they had no time for seeking additional employment. The result was shorter hours and higher wages for those landless women who did hire themselves out on other people's farms.

Table 1.1 Production Data for Selected Chandpur Region Crops, 1987

	Nonirrigated Villages	Irrigated Villages
Amon Paddy		
Percent of land to total land	38	93
Per acre yield of paddy (ton)	0.62	1.59
Value of paddy	3,400	8,600
Value of straw	167	350
Value of paddy and straw	3,567	8,950
Per acre yield of jute (ton)	0.46	n/a
Value of jute	2,500	n/a
Value of jute-stick	667	n/a
Total value of paddy, straw, jute, and jute-stick	6,734	n/a
Total operating cost	3,815	4,445
Net return	2,919	4,505
Wheat		
Percent of land to total land	23	3
Per acre yield (ton)	0.78	0.75
Value of wheat	5,040	4,860
Value of straw	150	150
Value of wheat and straw	5,190	5,010
Total operating cost	3,337	3,368
Net return	1,853	1,642
Boro Paddy		
Percent of land to total land	7	68
Per acre yield of paddy (ton)	1.56	1.85
Value of paddy	8,400	10,000
Value of straw	270	300
Value of paddy and straw	8,670	10,300
Total operating cost	5,780	5,722
Net return	2,890	4,678
Winter Vegetables and Spice		
Percent of land to total land	19	15
Value of produce	16,932	18,230
Per acre operating cost	7,767	8,285
Net return	9,165	9,945

Note: Values in takas per acre; n/a = not applicable.
Source: Chowdhury et al. (1989).

Because of their responsibility for postharvest activities, women in all of the four groups of landowning families experienced a dramatic increase in their work load resulting from the increases in production. Each woman had to adjust her time and working ability to meet the new volume of work. Employment of family labor in agriculture increased by 25 percent. On the other hand, the improved farm income allowed some men to hire

Table 1.2 Net Return per Acre, 1987 (in takas)

	Nonirrigated Villages	Irrigated Villages
Summer	2,860	4,389
Winter	4,502	4,906

Source: Chowdhury et al. (1989).

more workers, enabling them to move out of physical labor entirely.

The combination of higher levels of production and employment increased income for all families. However, higher costs for inputs and higher market prices offset much of this gain in real terms. Although farm employment for the landless increased, the plans for organizing their income earning through fishing did not materialize. In fact, the construction of a major embankment displaced those families that had relied on river fishing for their livelihoods. Wealthier families were able to use the increased water to construct ponds on their land, and the result was a shift in fish production and income from landless to landed people. Finally, landless people and tenants, even with increased incomes from labor, were unable to acquire land for themselves because the introduction of irrigation caused land prices to increase.

The most important impact of the CIP was on living conditions in the project area. The increased food supply meant that everyone was able to eat better, although not equally well. Those who previously ate one rice meal per day were able to afford two. Those who ate two could afford three. Patterns of food distribution in families did not change.

Improved paddy production also meant increased egg and poultry consumption. The paddy husk provided an excellent source of feed for chickens. Women involved in rice husking controlled this source of feed and began to raise poultry both for greater home consumption and for sale. The husbands and sons continued to do the marketing.

Families in the project area were found to spend ten times as much on home food consumption as their counterparts in nonirrigated nearby villages. This higher spending was necessary because the CIP villages had abandoned production of all winter crops except boro and had to buy winter food. Women in the non-CIP villages derived 20 percent of their income from vegetable sales, compared with only 5 percent for CIP village women.

The CIP area was plagued by fluctuations in electricity. In 1983 and 1986, electricity failures led to serious water shortages and consequent crop damage and loss. These failures continued to occur randomly, causing problems for farmers' planning.

Expectations for daughters and sons of CIP village people did not change, though spending for the education of boys did increase. Dowry requirements rose as well. Most gains in income were thus absorbed by increased expenses.

Case 2

India: Access to Schooling in Ambakach

NINAMA AND HEMA MET on the bus as they were returning from Ahmedabad to their villages. They were pleased—they had not seen each other since the time they had both been students at Teachers Training College. This had been in the early 1960s when the government was rapidly expanding its teaching force, taking people like Ninama and Hema who had only seventh standard education and giving them two years' training to become teachers in rural primary schools across India. During the more than twenty years since they had seen each other, Ninama had become a headmaster of a small school, and Hema, after teaching Standard 1 for many years, had joined the staff of an experimental nonformal education program.

As they talked, they discovered that each was returning to work after attending a family wedding. Ninama had stood in as the father for his nephew because his brother, the father of the groom, had died last year. It was good to see the young man marrying well, at age twenty-two, after that tragedy. Hema had been distressed to attend the marriage of her youngest niece, age seventeen, who seemed far too young to be taking on the responsibilities of marriage. Of course, Hema was the only member of her family who thought the girl too young—she was considered almost too old by her mother, who had married off the other six daughters when each reached fourteen.

"So, how is your work after these many years?" Ninama asked Hema as the bus bounced across the rural roads. Hema was clearly excited to

This case was adapted for teaching by Mary B. Anderson from Rao (April 1985) and Rao (March 1985).

answer. She began to describe the experimental nonformal education program she had joined as an in-service trainer. Children in the program ranged from eight to fourteen years of age, and the course lasted two years.

"We assume that children can learn effectively when they are trusted to discover their own way and style of learning," she said, "and we think that the failure of traditional primary schools lies partly in their inability to understand how poor and disadvantaged children learn." Hema explained that the experimental program concentrated on skills acquisition in language, mathematics, and reading and did not rely on the standard exam-based curriculum of the formal system. "Instead, the children use 'mastery learning techniques' that are designed to allow them to master a unit, each at his or her own pace, before proceeding to the next."

Teachers and pupils worked together, and the teacher was seen as a guide and supervisor of children's studies. As they sat in a circle together on the ground, the emphasis was on face-to-face interaction between teacher and students.

"We rely on community resources for the development of these schools. All our teachers are educated local people whom we continually train through visits—very few of them have over six or seven years of schooling themselves. Most of the men are farmers, and the women who become teachers in this program have been involved in housework full-time. We are developing a model of nonprofessional teachers who do not depend on teaching for their livelihood. They look on this service as a social duty. That is why the classes meet in homes or other village buildings at night, from 7 to 9, when all the people are free from their daily work. They only get paid a small honorarium of 50 rupees per month."

Though he nodded encouragingly and smiled, Ninama was silently disbelieving. His teachers earned an average of 750 rupees per month and often got discouraged by what seemed to be such low rewards for their hard work. And he knew the communities were really very similar.

Hema did not notice that Ninama was doubtful. She was warming to her subject, her eyes shining with enthusiasm. "The notion of a textbook as a permanently bound sheaf of pages—with a standard content for all pupils of all ages, abilities, and speeds of learning—has done great damage to education. Instead, we use an unbound set of units geared to individualized learning. These units include advanced and special interest materials suited to the varying interests and abilities of students and teachers. The project has prepared teaching-learning cards for practice, literacy primers, and plentiful supplementary reading materials specifically for these nonformal classes. We use the local vocabulary and speech styles of each area where we work and avoid the wholesale adoption of the urbanized standard regional languages that schools use."

Now Ninama had to speak. "That must cost a fortune to develop all those materials for local use!" he almost shouted.

"No. In the project classes, the books and aids are not individually owned, and no homework is assigned. All students and teachers share only two or three sets of materials, which reinforces a cooperative educational atmosphere and also reduces costs. We have an average class size of about fifteen. Overall, we estimate the per pupil cost for the supply of materials, including literacy primers, mathematics booklets and cards, science and other subject cards, and supplementary booklets, to range between 9 and 20 rupees over the two-year period each child attends. Our total project costs per child for completion of the course are 123 rupees, compared with the 960 rupees it costs to put a child through four years of primary schooling in the regular system."

Impressed in spite of himself and because he had admired Hema's intelligence and dedication ever since they were students together, Ninama asked his next question less skeptically. "So, what kinds of children come to this program? And how have they done? Is the project working as planned?"

"The children are poor. Their parents have not sent them to regular schools. Often they are a few years older than other children in the classes they would attend if they went to school. Yes, the program works. During the first three years of operation, we have had 4,242 students—3,238 girls and 1,004 boys. Our total dropout rate is 28 percent, which as you know is below the national average in the formal system, though it is still higher than we want. Forty-five girls and forty-one boys actually entered the formal system after they finished with us, continuing beyond Standard 4."

"Every year, we have a school fair. Each child performs for the whole community. The children sing, recite, do sums, tell stories from history— whatever they want to do to show off what they learned. Everyone loves it! Oh! And last year, many of the girls whose families won't let them continue in school began pressuring us to set up additional chances for them to study. We've responded by opening eight reading centers in project areas. These are like a library and study, open to people fifteen years and older, and they operate on the same principles as the evening classes. The village furnishes the accommodations and light, and the project gives 50 rupees per month to an instructor-librarian who keeps it open. We also supply reading materials."

Ninama was disappointed to notice that the bus was nearing his village of Ambakach and it was time to leave this conversation. As he climbed down and said good-bye to Hema, he said, "Well, it sounds good. But fortunately, we don't need such a program in my village since we started our incentives program. This program encourages all of our children to come to the regular primary school by giving them books, slates, meals, and even a food supplement for good attendance."

But as Ninama turned to acknowledge Hema's wave, he wondered to himself if what he had said was really true.

Ambakach Village

Ninama took leave of the other passengers disembarking from the bus. Most were men of Ambakach returning home for a few days from their wage employment in nearby larger towns. Many had to travel for employment because local opportunities for earning income were limited. Usually they were employed as construction workers. This was not the dry season, so migration was not as great as it would be later in the year. During extremely dry periods, over a third of the entire village population left to find work as construction or agricultural laborers in more prosperous districts of Gujarat.

Ambakach was a remote and isolated village, connected to the *taluka* (block) headquarters, fifty-eight kilometers away, by dirt road. The population was 1,003, consisting of 554 males and 449 females and including 238 children of primary school age (between six and nine or ten years old), 127 boys and 111 girls. The 114 households were scattered in clusters of three to four huts each. Everyone in the village, including Ninama, was of the same tribal group.

Farming was the main livelihood in the area, but the land was poor and water scarce. Of the 102 farmers in Ambakach, only nine owned more than ten hectares of land. Land distribution was as shown in Table 2.1.

Table 2.1   Land Distribution in Ambakach Village

Number of Farmers	Hectares of Land Owned
9	10 or more
38	5 to 10
32	2 to 5
23	1 to 2

Source: Rao (April 1985).

The agriculture in the area was rain-fed, and only one annual crop cycle was possible because of the poor soil quality. Thus, in terms of land size, this community was better off than some, but crop productivity was too low to support the families entirely. The area was extremely dry, and the land was strewn with rocks. Stumps of trees dotted the deforested landscape. The major crops were maize, lentils, and cattle fodder; a few farmers grew some wheat.

Livestock were very important in Ambakach, with farmers owning 197 bulls, 86 cows, 61 buffaloes, and 127 goats. Ambakach did not have its own milk cooperative, but was associated with one in an adjacent village.

Grazing the livestock was a job often assigned to young children, starting as early as six years of age. The village was quite poor. In the dry season, families could eat only one meal a day; it consisted primarily of maize, *dal,* and perhaps a chili or two. Few people grew any vegetables, and milk was not consumed except in tea or in yoghurt. Ambakach had no electricity, and the only drinking water well, located near the school, was not in use because people had no ropes or buckets to draw the water. Because cash was limited, they preferred fetching their water from the river. There were no shops, and the nearest primary health center was twenty-two kilometers away. Infant mortality was high.

As he walked the eight kilometers to his house, Ninama passed a number of the houses where the families of the students in his school lived. He thought about them and their families as he passed, pondering the circumstances that affected which children went to school and which did not. Many thoughts occurred to him:

> There's the home of Jamnaben. Her father is more educated than most people in this village. I think he finished seventh standard; he now works as a community health volunteer in a village some distance away. He told me once that he had to quit school because his family could not afford for him to continue. Therefore, he really wants his children to have as much education as he can give them. His older son is now in Standard 5 in the boarding school in Mandor. Her father wants Jamnaben to complete secondary school, but she has a long way to go—she's only in Standard 2 now. The other son is doing well in Standard 1 at our school.
>
> However, the older daughter is not in school. Her parents say they need her to graze their animals and to help with domestic work. I guess they do—besides, having three out of four children in school is pretty good for a family in this village. Anyway, she must be close to twelve or so, and most families insist that their girls leave coeducational school when they reach puberty.
>
> Now, there's a more typical household for this town—the household of Kokila. She is in Standard 2 in our school, but she is one of ten children. Four of her sisters are married, and two others help with the grazing of animals and household tasks. Their mother is too busy to do these things because she has to do almost all of the work on their meager farm.
>
> Eight girls! I wonder how they afford all those dowries to marry those girls? Sometimes I understand the arguments of parents who say they see no use in sending their girls to school. They just get married and go to live with their husbands' families anyway. Now, if parents could be sure their daughters would marry into better families if they were educated, that would be different. But in a village like this, it just isn't so.
>
> I think Kokila's other sister and a brother migrated to town in search of wage employment. They will probably pay the dowries for the two other girls and for Kokila. I remember also that the eldest brother dropped out of Standard 1 some years ago because the teacher beat him. But when his father died a few years ago, he assumed the role of head of the household and manages the family farm. The two sisters who take

care of the animals and household tasks are nearing marriage age. When they do get married and leave home, I am not sure Kokila will be able to stay in school. Her mother will probably need her at home. I remember when her neighbor, Bhuriaben, was pulled out of school just after Standard 2 because her father said he needed her to graze his four buffaloes. But when I talked with him last month, he said he would like to send her back to school if he could find someone else to tend his animals.

Ninama looked up from his musings and saw several of the mothers of his students. The women were on their way to fetch water in these late afternoon hours. Many were accompanied by their daughters who were no longer in school. The larger their families, the more the mothers relied on their daughters to help with this and the other many necessary household tasks. Older daughters helped care for their younger siblings and assisted with cooking, house cleaning, laundry, and postharvest storage of crops. Even very young girls were involved in some of these jobs, such as cleaning cooking pots and sweeping the household compound.

Men and older boys also worked in the fields during planting and harvesting seasons, but migrated during the dry seasons looking for wage employment. Many families tried very hard to educate at least one child, usually a boy, who could then find paid employment to help support the rest of the family. To get such a job, however, a high school education would be required, and some families were unable to keep a child in school this long.

When he got to school tomorrow, thought Ninama, he would look at the figures. He wondered exactly what the impact of the incentives program had been and whether it was really getting the children into school who should be there. He wondered how to analyze the success or failure of the incentives program.

School Incentives Program

In 1983, the chief minister of Gujarat singled out ten extremely poor tribal villages, among them Ambakach, for intensive development efforts under the tribal subplan. One aspect of the development program provided agricultural "inputs kits" for farmers. The kits included seeds and fertilizers and were provided initially for free and later at reduced costs.

Another program was the school incentives program, under which uniforms, textbooks, slates, classroom equipment, midday meals, and an allotment of food grains were provided to children in the villages. The purpose was to boost enrollments and attendance rates of the children in their primary schools.

Central and state government incentives for economically and socially disadvantaged students had been in effect for two decades in India. The Fourth All-India Educational Survey of 1978 had found that 26 percent of all rural primary schools were covered by a midday meal program; 12.5 percent had access to free uniforms; 38 percent received free textbooks; and scheduled caste and scheduled tribe girls in 38 percent of rural primary schools received scholarships for attending school.

Before the incentives program began in Ambakach, Ninama and the teachers had gone house to house, visiting parents and explaining the program. This was the first time they had made such visits in an organized way. Because they lived in the village, they often interacted informally with the families, making formal visits unnecessary.

There were two distinguishing characteristics of the special school incentives program begun in 1983 in the ten targeted villages. First, this program involved an effort to provide incentives to all eligible children. Second, it provided an additional monthly "grain package" to all children who maintained an 80 percent monthly attendance record in school. Girls who qualified received ten kilograms of corn each month, and boys received eight kilograms. Although these food allotments lasted most families for only four or five days, they constituted an important monthly supplement, especially in the dry season.

Ninama thought the grain distribution had worked especially well. On the days the grain was distributed, he sent the children home after lunch to call their parents to collect their shares. Three teachers supervised the grain distribution. When the program first began, all the eligible parents were called one by one and asked to put their thumb impressions on a list as a means of verifying their eligibility to the authorities. After that, each month when they arrived for the distribution, their names were verified, and the bags of grain were opened by two members of the village community. Distribution commenced. Two measures were used: one ten-kilogram measure and one eight-kilogram measure. Several parents with more than one child who attended school collected two or, sometimes, three shares. The atmosphere was always orderly and pleasant, with teachers joking with the villagers and villagers laughing and talking among themselves.

Sometimes parents whose children attended school irregularly arrived and wanted to receive a grain allotment. This gave the teachers an opportunity to explain that the families could not receive grain unless their children attended school 80 percent of the time.

Ninama thought that the uniform and textbook/slate distributions were also important. They were more variable, however, because although the grain allotments generally were received regularly and on time each month, the uniforms, books, and slates did not reach the school at any fixed time during the year. When they did come, sometimes only once or twice a year, the teachers simply decided which children needed them the most and distributed them accordingly.

Ninama realized that he should look into the impact of these incentives on school enrollments and attendance. He decided he would do so first thing tomorrow morning when school opened.

School in Ambakach

The next morning, as Ninama walked up the small hillock to the school at about 10:00, he noticed children already arriving in groups of twos and threes. School did not actually begin until 11:00 a.m., and it closed each day at 5:00 p.m. Children were eager to arrive, however, and he saw them coming across the fields with their slates and books tied up in small cloth satchels. He noticed that only about half of them wore uniforms and many of these were torn. At 11:00 a.m. sharp, the school bell rang, and all the children congregated in the single classroom, which was decorated with charts and colorful paper, for morning prayers and the national anthem. For the thousandth time, Ninama regretted the fact that the school had only one room. A contract for building an additional room had been awarded several years earlier, but after completing construction of only the foundation, the contractor had disappeared. The *taluka* development officer had promised Ninama that he would try to get the money to complete this room, but these things took time.

Having completed the prayers and anthem, the students dispersed to their alloted spaces: The first standard stayed in the classroom; the second went to the open space adjacent to the building; and the third and fourth went to opposite sides of the veranda. Two fourth standard boys who had been chosen for their neat handwriting began to enter the names of all children present in the daily register.

Ninama walked among the classes. In Standard 1, he saw that the one woman teacher in his school was exhorting her students to come to school with their faces washed and their hair combed. As she talked, she combed out the hair of the most disheveled students. Soon class was in order, with the youngest students seated on the floor shouting the poems they had memorized and the older children working in small groups on sums or writing and reading. Standard 1 was the largest class, with sixty boys and thirty-two girls.

The scenes in Standards 2 and 3 were not very different, except the male teachers did not spend time on the children's appearance. They sat at their desks or walked among the students, who sat in circles on the ground, and listened to recitations or taught new material. In the higher standards, the numbers enrolled diminished. Standard 2 had thirty-two boys and eight girls; Standard 3 had thirteen boys and three girls. Finally, Ninama went on to the class he taught, Standard 4, where he had fifteen boys and one girl this year.

As soon as he had a chance, Ninama asked his teachers to give him some figures that would help him assess the impact of the school in-

Table 2.2 Distribution of Attendance Incentives, by Gender and Standard

Incentives	September 1983–March 1984										September 1984–December 1984									
	Standard 1		Standard 2		Standard 3		Standard 4		Total		Standard 1		Standard 2		Standard 3		Standard 4		Total	
	M	F	M	F	M	F	M	F	M	F	M	F	M	F	M	F	M	F	M	F
Grain/Month																				
September	28	12	9	1	10	1	6	0	53	14	39	15	24	6	11	2	14	0	88	23
October	25	11	9	1	12	1	6	0	52	13	39	16	17	6	7	2	15	0	78	24
November	—	—	—	—	—	—	—	—	—	—	16	8	22	5	7	1	13	0	58	14
December	30	10	12	3	14	4	6	0	62	17	12	7	24	5	10	1	13	0	59	13
January	25	8	9	1	14	5	4	0	52	14										
February	27	11	9	2	13	4	5	0	54	17										
March	27	9	13	1	17	3	7	0	64	13										
Uniforms	30	12	7	0	14	2	8	1	59	15	—	—	32	4	13	3	15	1	60	8
Slates	25	10	—	—	—	—	—	—	25	10	—	—	15	0	—	—	—	—	15	0
Books	25	10	—	—	—	—	—	—	25	10	—	—	7	3	8	2	10	0	25	5

Source: Rao (April 1985).

centives program. Tables 2.2 through 2.4 summarize what they told him. He studied this data and drew Figure 2.1, which traced the retention rates of boys and girls in his school from 1982 to 1984. Then he asked himself how well the incentives program was working and whether there was anything he should do to make it work better.

Table 2.3   1982 Enrollment and 1983–84 Enrollment and Attendance, by Gender and Standard

		Enrollment Sept. 1982	Enrollment Sept. 1983	Monthly Average Attendance (1983–84) Sept.	Oct.	Nov.	Dec.	Jan.	Feb.	Mar.	Apr.
Standard 1	M	19	M 35	28	24	22	27	29	30	30	26
		23	51								
	F	4	F 16	12	12	9	12	9	12	10	8
Standard 2	M	19	M 18	9	9	13	13	12	13	13	10
		26	25								
	F	7	F 7	1	1	2	3	1	3	4	1
Standard 3	M	17	M 21	10	12	14	15	14	17	15	13
		23	28								
	F	6	F 7	1	1	1	5	4	5	7	2
Standard 4	M	16	M 13	6	6	8	8	8	8	8	6
		17	15								
	F	1	F 2	0	0	0	0	0	0	0	0
Total	M	71	M 87								
		89	119	67	65	69	83	77	88	87	66
	F	18	F 32								

Source: Rao (April 1985).

Table 2.4   1984–85 Enrollment and Attendance, by Gender and Standard

		Enrollment September 1984	Monthly Average Attendance September	October	November	December
Standard 1	M	60	40	46	44	45
		92				
	F	32	24	24	22	29
Standard 2	M	32	30	21	20	26
		40				
	F	8	7	7	6	6
Standard 3	M	13	11	12	7	8
		16				
	F	3	2	2	1	2
Standard 4	M	15	14	14	13	13
		16				
	F	1	0	0	0	0
Total	M	120				
		164	128	126	113	129
	F	44				

Source: Rao (April 1985).

Figure 2.1   Retention Rates of the 1982 Cohort, Ambakach Primary School

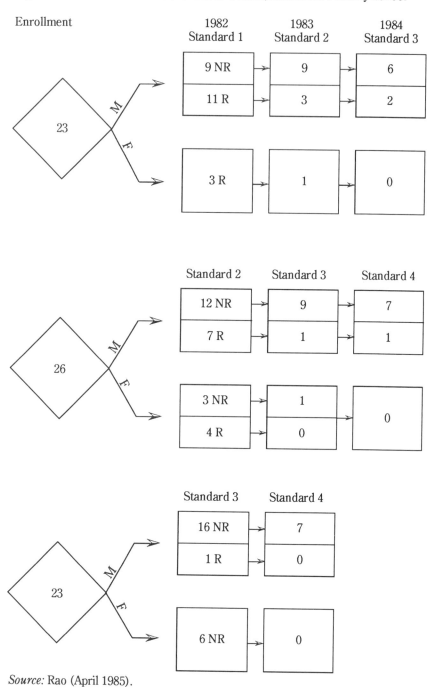

Source: Rao (April 1985).

Case 3

India: The Maharashtra Employment Guarantee Scheme

THE REGULAR MONTHLY MEETING of *taluka* (block level) administrators to review the workings of the Maharashtra employment guarantee scheme (EGS) was in progress. This particular morning in late April 1987, the meeting was not going as smoothly as usual. Sheela was disgusted. "Here in Maharashtra, we have the best employment guarantee scheme in all of India, yet all I hear is complaints! What do the people want, anyway? We give them guaranteed employment whenever they ask for it. We pay them at a fair wage. But my office has been full all week of people complaining. I'm fed up!"

"I'm having the same problem," said Anil. "It has been getting worse each year, but this year, because of the failed monsoon, the situation is out of hand. I am supposed to assign people to projects near home, but the technical departments are not coming up with projects to hire all the people demanding work. They tell me that they cannot start any projects in the foreseeable future within the five-kilometer radius of half of my villages. You know this makes much more work for me." So the meeting went, with each of the *taluka* leaders in the subdistrict reporting similar problems.

Mr. Gupta, the collector in charge of the EGS for this district, was attending the meeting that day. He was unusual among the district collectors whose job it was to oversee the EGS—he liked to meet with the people who actually ran the scheme whenever he had a chance. But he had

This case was adapted for teaching by Mary B. Anderson from Acharya and Panwalkar (1988) and Gupta et al. (1987).

been noticing an increasing dissatisfaction reported at these meetings in recent years.

Mr. Gupta had been involved with the EGS since its beginning in 1971, and listening to the *taluka* leaders around him now, he thought he should review the program in his district. Perhaps it did need some rethinking and some adjustments. He was well connected with the Ministry of Planning for Maharashtra State—the place where policy was set—and he knew that if he came up with valid suggestions for improving the program, the minister would be pleased.

Purpose and Workings of the EGS

Gupta remembered how the Maharashtra employment guarantee scheme was begun in the early 1970s in response to a severe drought that caused as much as a 35 percent failure in crops and left most agricultural workers jobless. Small and marginal farmers and landless people who depended on agricultural employment were desperate for alternative income opportunities. EGS began as a food-for-work crash program to meet the immediate needs of the rural population hardest hit by the drought.

In 1975, Maharashtra State passed the EGS Statutory Act, instituting the scheme in all districts. The act stated that every adult age eighteen and older had the right to work. Hence, the state undertook to employ all such persons in unskilled manual work, paying them on a weekly or fortnightly basis at a wage rate set in compliance with local wages.

The statutory EGS was intended to accomplish two things. First, it should provide gainful employment to every rural person (both men and women) in the state who required it. Second, it should create with this labor useful and productive assets in the state that would in turn help enhance overall productivity and improve the economic conditions of the state.

Eligibility for Employment

All rural persons over eighteen years of age were eligible for employment. In families without anyone over eighteen, persons over fifteen years of age could apply. Anyone wanting employment through the scheme was required to register with the relevant authorities at the village- or block-level offices. (A block is the smallest administrative unit of the state; it comprises 100–200 villages.) Once registered, individuals were given identity cards that they then had to present upon beginning any employment.

Conditions of Employment

Following is a list of some of the conditions and requirements of the EGS:

1. Only unskilled labor was guaranteed, and workers had no choice about the kind of work they were assigned.

2. The work would be provided within a five-kilometer radius of the village where the workers resided. If employment could only be provided at a greater distance, the government had to make arrangements for shelter, water, first aid, and access to ration shops for the workers at the site where work was offered.
3. Work should be provided within fifteen days after workers demanded it. If this was not possible, an unemployment compensation of 2 rupees (Rs) per day must be paid to each unemployed worker.
4. The wage bill should amount to 60 percent of the total costs of projects undertaken through the EGS. Thus, EGS projects were all labor-intensive. The 60 percent ratio was to be approximated in each project; it was strictly required at the aggregate level.
5. When fifty or more workers demanded work in any locality, and if they needed work for at least thirty days, a project to employ them had to be initiated. If the labor force fell short of what was needed to complete a project, the project could be closed down even though some workers might continue to need the employment it offered. If this occurred, the revenue department was responsible for redeploying the workers who still demanded work.

Wages

The government prepared EGS wage schedules for different types of work in different terrains and in different locations. The schedules were fixed to ensure that a person who worked for seven hours in a day would earn a wage equivalent to the local minimum wage rate. Wages were based on the quality and quantity of work, and certain types of employment were paid higher wages. (See Table 3.1.) Typically, men were preferred for heavy rock breaking and women for soil shifting. Wages were to be paid every one or two weeks, usually on the day preceding the day off. In some circumstances, wages would be paid in part in rupees and in part by a coupon that was redeemable at a ration store for goods in kind.

When the scheme began, wages were set below the going on-farm rate in order to ensure that the EGS did not compete with agriculture in attracting needed labor. Later, the EGS adopted the Maharashtra State minimum wage as its wage rate.

Administration

The EGS was implemented through a collaborative arrangement of the revenue and technical departments of government. Mr. Gupta, as district collector, had to coordinate with the other tiers of government—the state, the division, the subdistricts, and the *talukas*.

At the state level, EGS was controlled by the Ministry of Planning, which was responsible for drawing up the financial plans and for sanctioning project grants, on a quarterly basis, to the divisions and districts. A twenty-six-member council, composed of elected representatives from the

legislative assembly, some concerned persons (including at least two people from the "scheduled" castes), and some appointed officials, reviewed
the program and ensured that the broad provisions for public participation
were maintained.

Table 3.1   1985 Wage Schedule (Rs) for Selected EGS Tasks

Task	Maximum Wage	Minimum Wage
Wage paid for 1 cubic meter digging and shifting to a 10-meter distance:		
Soft soil/soft earth	4.57	2.40
Hard earth with stones	8.43	4.40
Rocky soil/soft stones	19.16	10.00
Wet soil	6.70	3.50
Headload carrying of all types of soils/stones per cubic meter:		
10–80 meters distance	1.16	0.60
80–150 meters distance	1.33	0.70
Stone quarry work (manually cutting stone and heaping)	28.75	15.00
Shifting soil and dumping at a distance of 10 meters	5.57	2.90
Transplanting saplings (per 100 polythene bags)	2.91	1.50

Note: The EGS wage corresponds to the market rate in a given region. A *maxi-
mum* rate applies to the hilly areas of the coastal region around Bombay. Wages in
this area have been pushed up by proximity to the metropolis. *Minimum* wages
apply to the nonhilly areas of the eastern region of the state. Though this is a fer-
tile forest region, it has the lowest wage rate and least economic activity. It is populated mostly by tribals.
Source: Acharya and Panwalkar (1988).

But the most important level of planning and implementation for EGS
was the district level, where Mr. Gupta and other collectors who were revenue department officials had primary responsibility. It was the collector's
responsibility to prepare the plan of projects (known as the *blueprint*) to be
undertaken in the district, to delegate the financial and administrative
responsibilities for initiating the work to the appropriate technical departments (depending on the type of work to be done), and to assess the
demand for work on a periodic basis so that new projects could be started
when warranted.

The assessment of the demand for work was done jointly by the collector and officers of the revenue department at the subdivision and *taluka* levels. There are four or five subdivisions in a district and three or four *talukas* in a subdivision. These people, because of their familiarity with the villages from which the workers came, were able to assess the demand both seasonally and spatially. They also maintained financial and other records for their areas. The *taluka* administrator also was responsible for assigning people in his or her jurisdiction to work projects.

A district council, similar to that at the state level, was in charge of overseeing these activities at the district level. At the *taluka* level, the administrator coordinated with a local works committee made up of local politicians and two workers' representatives, one man and one woman.

Technical agencies of government were responsible for choosing project sites, drawing up the engineering designs, selecting and arranging for material and supplies, and certifying the completion of projects. Junior engineers, agricultural assistants, and forest conservators actually executed the projects by identifying the different tasks to be done in any project, ordering them in sequence and assigning the work to gangs of ten to fifteen workers. They appointed "mustering assistants" from nearby communities who would call the muster twice a day.

Work was assigned to gangs of workers rather than to individual laborers. Workers were often paid as a gang, with each member of the gang receiving equal wages. Most gangs were made up either of men or of women; seldom did they work in the same group.

Technical reports on progress were prepared weekly and submitted by the field officers to the technical departments. Attendance and expenditure totals were submitted to the *taluka* administrator every two weeks. These constituted the primary records of employment generated through the scheme and of costs incurred. Projects were certified as completed by the technical department concerned and then turned over to a district development administration body that was to maintain and use the assets created. This body was supposed to ensure that the assets were productive and to assess their value to the targeted beneficiaries.

How the EGS Worked

When it began, the EGS had a budget of Rs 22.3 million, but Mr. Gupta knew that in 1984–85, this had risen to nearly Rs 2,000 million. Between 1975 and 1985, over 161,000 projects were started with EGS funds, and about 68 percent of these were completed (Table 3.2). Total annual persondays of work created by EGS increased from 99 million in 1975 to 178 million in 1985. In 1985, the average monthly labor participation numbered 597,599, but there was quite a fluctuation over the seasons so that the difference between the highest and lowest monthly involvement was 300,000.

Table 3.2   Number and Types of EGS Projects, 1975–85

Project		Number of Projects Sanctioned (S)/Completed (C)	Percentage of Projects Completed
Soil conservation	S	92,645	81.3
	C	75,352	
Road works	S	19,042	39.5
	C	7,526	
Land development	S	17,248	62.1
	C	10,707	
Percolation tanks	S	9,693	47.9
	C	4,647	
Afforestation	S	8,790	43.8
	C	3,852	
Minor irrigation	S	7,772	52.9
	C	4,117	
Major irrigation (labor-	S	4,090	73.1
intensive component)	C	2,991	
Medium irrigation (labor-	S	871	47.6
intensive component)	C	415	
Other	S	1,289	57.3
	C	739	
Total	S	161,440	68.3
	C	110,346	

Source: Acharya and Panwalkar (1988, 15).

Table 3.3   Male and Female Participation in EGS Project

Year	Male Workers	Female Workers
1978–79	506,881	387,088
1979–80	562,725	391,045
1980–81	548,859	326,513
1981–82	370,945	433,963
1982–83	363,112	457,509
1983–84	218,792	254,867
1984–85	232,152	280,409

Source: Acharya and Panwalkar (1988).

Table 3.4   EGS Wages (Rs) for Given Years

Year	Wage/Person-day
1976–77	2.87
1977 78	3.30
1978–79	3.61
1979–80	4.36
1980–81	5.40

Year	Wage/Person-day
1981–82	6.28
1982–83	7.80
1983–84	8.41
1984–85	8.30

Source: Acharya and Panwalkar (1988).

Table 3.5   Rural Wages (Rs) in Maharashtra by Gender, 1972–73 and 1983

Year	Nominal Wage		Real Wage (adjusted to 1973 prices)
1972–73	M	2.29	2.29
	F	1.41	1.41
1983	M	6.15	3.14
	F	3.93	2.01

Source: Acharya and Panwalkar (1988).

Table 3.6   Average Daily Earnings (Rs) by Casual Wage Laborers in Rural Maharashtra

Occupation	Males	Females
Casual labor in public works programs	6.38	4.86
Casual labor in agriculture	6.09	3.86

Source: Acharya and Panwalkar (1988).

Table 3.7   Percentage Distribution of Persons by Number of Days Worked per Year in EGS and Non-EGS Activities

	EGS Households				Non-EGS Households	
	EGS Work		Non-EGS Work		Non-EGS Work	
Number of Days Worked	M	F	M	F	M	F
0–60	70.2	68.1	8.5	6.4	6.1	6.1
61–120	25.5	6.4	38.3	46.8	4.1	12.2
121–200	4.3	25.5	34.0	29.8	14.3	14.3
201 +	0.0	0.0	19.1	17.0	75.5	67.3
	100.0	100.0	100.0	100.0	100.0	100.0
Mean Days Worked	54.7	65.0	143.9	148.7	240.0	212.8
Total Days	M		F		M	F
Worked	198.6		213.7		240.0	212.8

Source: Acharya and Panwalkar (1988).

Table 3.8   Average Daily Wage (Rs) in EGS and Non-EGS Jobs

	EGS Activities Male	EGS Activities Female	Non-EGS Activities Male	Non-EGS Activities Female
Mean	5.28	5.33	5.61	5.55
Highest value	7.00	7.00	10.00	10.00
Lowest value	2.50	2.50	3.00	2.50

Source: Acharya and Panwalkar (1988).

Mr. Gupta also studied planning department statistics showing that in 1983, EGS generated 166 million person-days of employment, or about 60 percent of total nonagricultural casual employment in rural Maharashtra. Knowing both the number of people employed and the ratio of nonagricultural casual to total employment (14:100), he was surprised when he calculated that EGS contributed less than 3 percent of the total rural employment during that year.

Gupta was interested in pursuing the issue of the EGS's effectiveness. He looked through his files, locating additional figures for employment, wages, earnings, and so on for the program. He organized them into Tables 3.3 through 3.8. After studying this information, Mr. Gupta decided to accompany Sheela to a village in her *taluka.* He wanted to find out from the workers how they felt about the EGS. First, he reviewed what he knew about the people's lives in Maharashtra.

Maharashtra State

Maharashtra State is in western India. It is densely populated, with about 160 persons per square kilometer. The majority of the people rely in part on agricultural employment, but about 15 percent of the labor force is involved in nonagricultural activities such as shopkeeping, artisan activity, and nonfarm labor.

Because the area is largely semiarid, agricultural production is unstable and depends on the rains each year. The vagaries of the monsoon force people to hire out their labor in construction activities or as casual day laborers on farms. About 35 percent of the rural population of Maharashtra is below the poverty line (defined as below 2,250 caloric intake per day). Small marginal farmers and the landless constitute over 50 percent of the rural population.

Population in rural Maharashtra grew at a rate of 20.43 percent between 1971 and 1981, even though there was simultaneously a substantial migration to urban areas. The number of workers increased by about 17 percent, the increase in male workers being about 19 percent and in female workers just under 15 percent.

The size of landholdings decreased as a result of the increase in population. In 1971, the average landholding was 4.25 hectares; by the end of the decade, average landholding size was only 2.95 hectares. The cultivated area per person employed in agriculture fell from 1.16 hectares to about 1.03 hectares. This had an impact on labor allocations of families: When landholdings are small, men continue to work on their own land, whereas women of the household, as redundant labor on their own small plots, hire themselves out to work on other people's farms or in other income-generating projects.

Productivity of land rose over the same period, primarily because of increased use of high-yielding technologies, especially irrigation in some areas. It rose from 0.44 metric tons to about 0.70 metric tons of food grains per hectare.

In Maharashtra, the monsoon crop is grown between July and September, and thus most people are occupied during this time in agriculture. When this crop is harvested, the winter crop is sown. Between March and June, however, there is little crop-related activity, and the incidence of unemployment is high.

Mr. Gupta and Sheela were visiting the village during late April. Not only was this the normal slack period for agricultural employment, but this year the monsoon had been poor, leaving even more people unemployed.

The Village

By interviewing Sheela and the village leaders when he arrived, Mr. Gupta put together a clear picture of life in this area.

Agriculture

He found that over 90 percent of the villagers earned their livelihoods through agriculture, but at best it did not provide a sufficient income to support their families. Thus, almost every family resorted to some other kind of work for wages to sustain themselves. Those from the village who were educated and semiliterate had long since migrated to the larger towns of Maharashtra (Bombay and Pune) to work in textile mills and engineering companies. Some also worked there as casual day laborers. During the dry season, one option each family had was to send some family members to the cities for day labor. Many families found this to be their only way to survive, and in some cases, entire families migrated either to cities or other farming areas during this period.

Within the village, families divided the agricultural work among their members. Men did most of the land preparation, plowing, and other heavy work. Women were responsible for weeding, harvesting, and winnowing the crops. Because women were pretty much tied to their home areas, they did not ordinarily take their crops to the market for sale; this was the responsibility of men.

One of the men from the village told Mr. Gupta: "Women take more pains with their work; they are working continuously. They work on farms or on-site, and after coming back from work, they have work at home waiting for them." Sheela told him that women rise before the sun to light the fire and fix *chappatis* (flat baked bread) for the family. They sweep the compound, fetch the water, and get each family member up and fed to start the day. Of course, they prepare all meals and do whatever cleaning is necessary.

In families that had cattle, usually goats and cows, women and girls often handled the grazing. This task could also be assigned to boys or to a professional grazer who was paid a fee. Sometimes men took the animals out to graze. It was the job of women and girls to gather dung for fuel or fertilizer. Sometimes they used it in their own households; usually they sold it for income.

Women, especially the wives of men who migrated to find employment on a seasonal basis, made a number of the household decisions. They decided when and what to sow, what household items needed to be bought, and, in the case of their own wage labor, when and where to go out of the household to work.

Education in the village was limited because all families were so poor that they needed their children to work to help support the family. Most boys and girls went to school in their early years, before they were really able to provide much income-earning assistance. Both were taken out of school when they were old enough to do other work, but girls were more often removed from school because they were important contributors to the running of the household and took care of younger siblings.

The people told Mr. Gupta how difficult a decision this was for them to make. They said that they value education and see it as a way to increase total family income and security, but that the current pressures forced them to take the short view—putting children to work now—rather than the long view that would allow them to keep their children in school in hopes of their earning more in the future.

Water was the primary problem in this village, as was true in most other villages in the area. There was a community well that yielded water only between August and March. An engineer who visited the village for a voluntary agency three years earlier had indicated that he thought this well could be made to yield water year-round if it were deepened, lined, and covered. A bore-well constructed in the 1970s had dried up. A hand pump on it broke soon after installation, and the government finally removed it.

More serious than the problem of water for household consumption, however, was the problem of irrigation. Agriculture was unable to sustain family consumption because all cultivation depends on rain, and when the rain came, there was no system for retention or storage. All of the investments required to control water were beyond the village capacity. Although the people often talked of the importance of irrigation, none of them knew how to begin to initiate a project to build the system. The village also needed a better road to connect it to the nearest markets, about seven kilometers away.

EGS in the Village

The villagers told Mr. Gupta that the employment guarantee scheme provided needed employment in the village. Between June and October, most families worked on EGS projects. Sheela told him that, on average, four people from each family participated in the EGS.

The previous year, people had worked on an EGS job about six kilometers away building bunds, work that involved digging, carrying, and filling. They formed themselves into work groups of two to three members because they found this size of work group most efficient. They earned about Rs 5 per day per person.

These workers said the bund had since fallen into disrepair, but that was all right in their opinion because they knew they could again be hired to repair it someday. This was the usual pattern. They worked on the building of something, then were later hired to repair it. Only when the asset they worked on was used by some of the large landholders to increase their productivity was it kept in good condition.

Now the government was sponsoring the building of a percolation tank nearby. A private contractor was in charge of the project, and 150 people were employed full-time as workers.

The contractor told Mr. Gupta that he kept a daily record of who was employed. Mr. Gupta asked to see this record, but the contractor would not provide it. He continued to describe his system for record keeping. He said that he gave each worker a token each day according to the work the person put in. He was reluctant to hire women for the heavy work because it was not right that women should do these tasks. He paid Rs 8 per day for heavy work, Rs 5–6 per day for light work. Often he did not get his money from the government in time to pay the workers on the regular fifteen-day schedule. He sometimes hired children, though he was not supposed to do so. They came with their mothers to the work site, and he thought that so long as they were there, they might as well do some of the carrying. He did not have to keep any records on them, and he could pay them at a piecework rate for whatever they did. Their mothers were very happy to have even a few rupees earned by their children. His average wage bill per worker was about Rs 5 per day.

Sometimes the contractor paid the workers with coupons redeemable for goods, grain, and oils in the nearby store. He had heard that the storekeeper sometimes refused these, but that was not his problem. He was just following government regulations about payment. He said he found it easier to pay the lump sum of several people's work to one worker and leave it to that person to distribute the appropriate amounts among the coworkers. He also loaned money to his workers in advance of their wages because, he said, he knew they had a hard time surviving between pay periods. He charged the usual interest rate of the village money lender. He said that he had very few complaints from his workers about low wages or the poor quality of cereals paid to them.

Mr. Gupta compared the work available to these villagers through the EGS and through agriculture (Tables 3.9 and 3.10). With this and the other information he had assembled, he thought he now had a better picture of the workings of the EGS. He sat down to write a memorandum to the Ministry of Planning, suggesting certain changes and improvements.

Table 3.9   EGS Employment for Representative Years

Year	Nature of Work	Wage Rate (Rs)/Week
1980	Percolation Tank	30–36 + 6 kg. wheat
1982	Road Construction	35–36 + 6 kg. wheat
1983	Percolation Tank	40–50
1984	Percolation Tank	40–50
1985	Percolation Tank and Road Construction	45–50

Source: Village Profiles, Maharashtra, compiled by field researchers for Gupta et al. (1987).

Table 3.10   Employment Available on Farm

Month	Nature of Work	Wage Rate (Rs)/Day Male	Female
May–July	Potato planting/harvesting	12	6
June–August	Sugarcane planting/harvesting	11–12	6–7
August	Bajra harvesting	12	6
July–August	Weeding	—	6–7

Source: Village Profiles, Maharashtra, compiled by field researchers for Gupta et al. (1987).

Case 4

Indonesia: The P2WIK-UNDP Batik Project

THE ARCHIPELAGO OF 13,667 islands in the Indian and Pacific oceans forms the Republic of Indonesia. It is the largest and most populous country in Southeast Asia. In 1985, the population totaled 173 million. The island of Java, which comprises only 7 percent of the country's land mass, was home to 60 percent of Indonesia's population.

Agriculture is the principal source of livelihood in rural Indonesia and the most important sector of the Indonesian economy. It employs over half of the labor force and contributes more than 25 percent to gross domestic product. The Green Revolution was remarkably successful in increasing rice production, especially on Java. The introduction of high-yielding rice varieties along with chemical fertilizers and pesticides and the increase in multiple cropping of irrigated fields increased rice production from 12.2 million tons in 1969 to 26.3 million tons in 1985.

The introduction of other technologies has led to changes in the agricultural sector. The traditional harvesting system in which large groups of women harvested rice using a hand-held blade in exchange for a share of the yield has been replaced by a contract labor system. A middleman now hires small groups of men and/or women for a daily wage. The adoption of the sickle for harvesting, used only by men, has reduced overall labor requirements and limited the traditional employment opportunities for women. The introduction of the mechanical rice huller has replaced hand pounding of rice, a task traditionally performed by women for payment. At the same time, monetization of labor relationships has increased the need for money.

This case was adapted for teaching by Catherine Overholt from Joseph (1987).

Over three-quarters of all farmers own less than half a hectare of land. Increased productivity has enabled larger farmers to buy out smaller farmers, leading to increased landlessness. Perhaps a third of the population of Java is landless. Increasing landlessness has led to male outmigration, as men seek employment in the urban informal sector or in semi- and unskilled jobs in industry and construction. Small and intermittent contributions to family income made by men reflect the limited types of employment available to them.

The number of female-headed households has grown. It is estimated that 16 percent of all households are headed by women, and rates are slightly higher in rural areas: 15 percent of rural women are married, but the husband is absent; 13 percent are divorced. Over 74 percent of all divorcees were found to be economically active. Of these, 32 percent were able to support a single person's need, but 49 percent were unable to earn enough to support themselves.

Despite impressive improvements in per capita income since 1970, poverty remains a major Indonesian problem. In 1981, per capita GNP was estimated at 464,385 rupiah (Rp), or $415. Yet nearly 60 percent of the population was living below the absolute poverty line.

Village life has changed very little over the years for the three-fourths of the population who still reside in rural areas. As has been the case for centuries, the lives of most people revolve around rice cultivation. Their actions are guided by *adat* (common or customary law), which has evolved from ancient times when villages were self-governing.

On Java, women share the same rights as men with respect to marriage, divorce, inheritance, and property rights. Women have a considerable degree of economic independence and initiative, exercise social power, and traditionally hold high status. Female children bring economic benefits because they provide labor and bring a bride price. The Javanese wife enjoys equal status in household decision-making regarding both production and consumption issues. Woman are described as being the silent head of household (has the "informal" power), and the husband is the family representative (has the "formal" power). All income is turned over to the wife, and she decides how it will be spent, consulting her husband on major purchases. Many families, therefore, are dependent on the wife's financial capabilities.

Although women enjoy high status, they do not always share equally in opportunities. Government efforts during the 1970s eradicated the gap between male and female primary school attendance. However, use of girls' labor for family and household work contributes to higher female school absenteeism and dropout rates. In addition, many villages have no schools beyond primary level, and children therefore must leave the village and enter a boarding facility to continue higher education.

Employment opportunities for women in agriculture have decreased dramatically. Alternative employment is severely limited and varies with educational levels achieved. However, one-third to almost one-half of all women between the ages of fifteen and sixty-five in rural areas are engaged in some type of paid employment.

Peran ganda is an ideology that defines suitable women's work according to "natural" abilities (e.g., mothering) and innate characteristics (e.g., patience, attention to detail). The assertion is that women are not suited to certain types of work or production processes, and government policies and programs contain guidelines that reflect this view: "The role of women in development expands in accordance with and in harmony with the widening of their responsibility and role in bringing into being and developing a healthy and prosperous family." This dual role of women is institutionalized in the popular belief that the current gender-based division of labor among middle and upper classes is both desirable and inalterable. Government programs tend to stress areas related to women's role as homemaker and socialization agent and employment opportunities that will not conflict with this role.

On Java, the decline of labor absorption in the agricultural sector and the demand for female labor has forced land-poor women in rural areas to seek income from other sectors of the economy. Official statistics estimated that the island's work force of 40.2 million included more than 12 million women and girls. The Indonesian government moved to implement programs aimed at increasing nonfarm employment opportunities for rural women. Batik making is an obvious choice for poor rural women and planners alike because of its acceptability in Javanese villages as women's work.

Batik Production

Batik, a wax-resist technique used to embellish textiles for everyday and ceremonial use, has been known in Indonesia in its present hand-drawn (*tulis*) form for more than 700 years. Whether the technique diffused from India or China or had indigenous roots in the Indonesian archipelago continues to be the subject of scholarly debate. Batik in its most refined form is considered by the Javanese to be a fine art capable of transferring cosmic power to the owner/wearer. Batik motifs traditionally indicate the wearer's status. In Central Java, the royal court issued rules specifying who was permitted to wear which, if any, batik patterns. Batik also is a widely practiced folk art. Powerful symbols drawn from Javanese religion, from elements of the local environment, and from foreign motifs are incorporated in highly stylized forms into attractive garments.

Batik has been produced by groups of women for personal use and as an occupation for at least two hundred years. Home-based batik production was geared to the peasant economy and closely related to the agricultural cycle. Production was part-time during slack agricultural periods or developed as cottage industry when farming alone did not meet subsistence needs. Until the middle of the nineteenth century, Javanese batik making consisted of cottage industries in rural areas and small-scale production under court patronage in some urban centers. Changes in Dutch colonial policies after 1850 led to commercialization of batik making through a factory-based production system and to the introduction of hand-stamped batik, features that increased productivity and lowered production costs. Modern Indonesian batik is usually described by the method of production, the quality of the finished product, or both. *Batik tulis* (see Appendix 4A at end of chapter) refers to batik made by applying wax to cloth with a penlike tool called a *canting*. *Batik cap* is produced by using copper stamps (*cap*) to imprint wax on the cloth. *Batik tulis* and *batik cap* are hand-production techniques. For this reason, they are often referred to as handmade, genuine, or real batik (*batik asli*). The terms *textile bermotif batik* and *batik printing* denote all facsimile fabric regardless of the technique used in their production. *Kombinasi,* as the name suggests, refers to combinations of techniques. The most common combination is *tulis* and *cap*, but mixtures of *cap* and printing and even *tulis* and printing are available on the domestic market.

Quality categorizations are determined by a variety of factors, including design, raw materials used, harmony of colors, and execution of the wax resist. Traditionally, the last consideration is the most important. The three gradations of batik—*hulus, sedang,* and *kasar*—roughly correspond to high, medium, and low, respectively. These terms are not comparable across batik types. Batik printing in particular cannot be evaluated in the same way because wax-resist techniques are not used. In general, these textiles are judged in terms of closeness in appearance to the original for traditional patterns and overall design for contemporary ones.

The two sets of descriptive terms are frequently combined. Such combinations are possible because one set of terms differentiates types of batik according to the production process, while the other set compares quality of individual pieces of batik produced by a particular process. *Batik tulis kasar,* for example, refers to low-quality batik made with a *canting*.

Batik *cap* increased productivity and lowered production costs. One person could stamp twenty *kain* (2.5 x 1 meter cloth) in one working day compared to one week to three months required for waxing one batik *tulis kain*. The use of home workers for some tasks reduced work space requirements and allowed wage differentiation for part-time work. In 1985, home workers earned 125 rupiah (Rp), or U.S. $0.11, for *kasar* quality and Rp 500 for *halus* quality; factory workers earned double these amounts. The returns to labor from cottage batik *tulis* industries have not been profitable for rural households. The influx into rural areas of relatively high-quality, inexpensive textiles from other regions reduced local demand for cottage batik industry products.

Factory production is larger-scale than home-based production and depends on hired labor. Tasks are gender-specific (Table 4.1, at end of chapter), and skill is the basis for remuneration. Three divisions are made: *cap* workers constitute *skilled* labor; dyers and boilers are considered *semi-skilled*; *canting* workers are *trained* labor. Men are recruited for stamping and dyeing because these tasks are considered heavy jobs unsuitable for women. Women and children are employed in urban enterprises and as home workers to do *canting* and cloth preparation. The division of labor in traditional batik production was based on heredity and class, and batik making was considered a low-prestige activity for men.

The most important determinant of overall quality and price of traditional batik is the fineness of the wax resist. Specialized skills must be developed in order to use the *canting* and *cap* well. Learning to use the *canting* takes anywhere from several months to acquire rudimentary skills to ten or more years to achieve the control necessary to make the finest batik *halus*. Girls begin making batik when they are five to seven years old. With proper discipline, they can make fine-quality batik by age fifteen. Girls are more likely to leave school to become batik workers because they become wage earners almost immediately. Boys begin learning *cap* work as soon as they are strong enough to work with the heavy metal stamps. Before that they may help with painting, rinsing, and other steps in the production process that do not require great physical strength. Boys working in the batik industry at early ages are often unpaid family labor since they are too young to handle the *cap* and rarely do *canting*.

Today nearly all batik *tulis* and batik *cap* fabric is produced by small-scale (5–19 employees) or medium-sized (20–100 employees) factories. Factory enterprises include home-based workers who generally are rural and are contracted by middlepeople to do piecework for urban enterprises in what is called the putting-out system.

The putting-out system is widely used to employ rural women in their homes and keep production costs low by both urban enterprises specializing in batik *tulis* and by rural batik *tulis* and batik *cap* production enterprises. Urban entrepreneurs supply materials, either raw materials or once-dyed cloth, to rural middlewomen. These middlewomen distribute the materials in their village, collect the completed work, and return it to the entrepreneur. The middlewoman receives partial payment for the work completed and a new supply of inputs. The middleperson obtains any materials, such as wax, not supplied by the entrepreneur.

Urban batik enterprises are far more numerous than rural ones, but the majority of batik workers are rural women employed by middlewomen in the putting-out system. In recent years, the expansion of mass transportation between rural and city areas has led workers to bypass the middleperson in favor of a direct trading relationship with the entrepreneur, though this arrangement is not without risk. Individual output is not enough to maintain connections with more than one or two entrepreneurs, and an entrepreneur who decreases production can leave an individual without work.

The batik industry relies on a two-tiered marketing system. Women predominate at the local level as middlepeople and traders, but the quantities of batik they handle are often small. In contrast, extraregional trade, in which larger quantities of batik are transported over long distances, is dominated by men.

Large-scale Batik Enterprises

Growth-oriented industrialization policies introduced in the early 1970s have supported the expansion of large-scale batik enterprises and a formidable capital-intensive pseudobatik industry. These industries produce batik and have their own spinning, weaving, batik printing, and ready-to-wear subdivisions. Batik *tulis* and *cap* constitute only a small part of their total production. Batik printing is their most important product for both domestic and export markets.

The company PT Batik Keris provides an example of large-scale batik and pseudobatik production. Batik Keris benefited from the government's policy shift away from protection of small-scale industries in favor of free trade. It expanded through use of extensive credit and tax incentives, growing from an industry that employed fifty workers to one that includes over a dozen factories, one of which employs 1,000 workers in three shifts. It has a diverse product line, including pseudobatik in yardage and traditional lengths, batik *cap* T-shirts, and batik *tulis* silk kimonos for the Japanese market. It hires a large number of designers who produce new designs about every three months. The company's influence over fashion trends is so great that its labels are sometimes forged. Batik Keris experiences only a 12 percent difference in production between highest and lowest demand periods compared with 75 percent fluctuations in small-scale enterprises.

The expansion of large-scale batik and pseudobatik producers has brought major structural changes to the batik industry. The impact of these changes has been felt most strongly by workers in small- to medium-scale enterprises. Market competition and labor displacement have become major issues. The Department of Industry reports that in Yogyakarta, only 10 percent of the batik factories registered in 1970 were still operating in 1984. A similar situation exists in Solo. Large-scale enterprises often prefer to subcontract work to rural women because the rate of pay is lower. The capital-intensive nature of the batik printing process and the extensive use of subcontracting by the batik giants have reduced employment opportunities and created job competition.

Batik-Making Households

Households on Java, including those of batik workers, generally consist of a nuclear family occasionally enlarged by a grandparent or other relatives. Rural households have an average of 2.9 income earners; urban households have 2.1. Rural batik workers employed in urban enterprises often live at the production site during the week. Most are young, unmarried women. Once married, women return to the village and continue as home-based workers. Remittances to the family can be quite significant; unmarried women may contribute as much as 70 percent of their income to their families. In early 1985, total household income for rural and urban batik workers' families was Rp 63,780 (U.S. $57) and Rp 53,160 per month respectively. Other information regarding batik-making households is presented in Tables 4.2 through 4.8 at the end of the chapter.

P2WIK-UNDP Project in Wukirsari

Five government departments are involved in the development of small-scale industries: the Departments of Industry, Trade, Cooperatives, and Labor and the Office of the Minister for the Development of the Role of Women. The Department of Industry through its Directorate General of Small-scale Industries is the most active. Cottage industries are defined as those with 1 to 4 family members engaged in home-based production. Small-scale industries are those that employ 5 to 19 workers as paid or unpaid labor. These two industry categories were expected to grow at 6 percent per annum during the Fourth Five-Year Plan (1984–1989). Government policies were designed to encourage labor-intensive small-scale enterprises that produce goods in high demand in the domestic market.

Since 1981, the Directorate General of Small-scale Industries in conjunction with the Office of Minister for the Development of the Role of Women has operated P2WIK, a national program funded primarily by the United Nations Development Program (UNDP) to assist women in cottage industries. The purpose of P2WIK was to integrate rural women into the development process and increase family income. It operated in all twenty-seven provinces as a subdivision of the family welfare program, P2W-KSS. The government was actively attempting to revive home-based batik industries because it recognized the need for off-farm employment in rural areas and the importance of poor rural women's earnings to their families' income.

The P2WIK-UNDP project was established by the Department of Industry to enable local women to become independent batik producers. It was conceived as a community development project with the aim of upgrading women's batik-making activities and helping them become small-scale batik entrepreneurs. Its primary goal was to raise participants' income, and poor women were the target group. Secondary goals included increasing product quality and production, developing cooperation among group members, and expanding marketing networks to retail outlets both within and beyond the region. Initially, the project planned to involve 288 women in 12 villages. By 1984, the unofficial number was twice that many. Planning takes place at the central and regional levels, with local "motivators" trained to act as liaisons between project participants and government officials. The program was coordinated with other village-level development projects. From 1981 to 1984, UNDP contributed U.S. $500,000 to the program. The Indonesian government provided an additional U.S. $32,000 in 1982–1983.

Wukirsari, eighteen kilometers south of Yogyakarta, was one of twelve villages in nine provinces chosen for a P2WIK-UNDP project. It was within an official poverty area (1984 per capita income Rp 150,000). Twenty-one percent of the 2,426 households were headed by women. Less than half of the village households owned any land, and those that did owned plots. Only one household owned more than 0.5 hectares of wet rice land; only 25 owned more than 0.5 hectares of dry fields. Because of its location at the edge of a major limestone formation, most land was ill suited to intensive cultivation. Farming did not provide sufficient income for most households. However, a number of small-scale industries employed local residents, and a large number of households engaged in batik making.

Peasant women in the area had long been involved in making traditional textiles. The village produced only semifinished batik *tulis* until a few years before. Batik makers with capital to invest in wages and raw materials became middlewomen. They recruited and trained home-based workers and carried finished textiles to entrepreneurs in Imogiri and Yogyakarta. The higher wages attracted both men and women into home-based batik making, but men stopped doing *canting* work around 1980 when employment as casual and semi-skilled laborers became available in the city. Middlewomen in Wukirsari pay workers in full on completion of each piece and do not withhold wages for too long because their workers are also relatives and neighbors. There are a number of middlewomen for each quality product, and workers are free to take work from whomever they choose.

Twenty-six women from Wukirsari were chosen by the village headman and his wife (also the director of the local PKK, the national Healthy and Prosperous Family Program) to participate in the P2WIK-UNDP project. Two high school graduates who were active in community affairs were recruited as motivators and sent to Jakarta for training in cooperative management and basic business skills. The women were organized into a *kelompok,* a cooperative-type group, with a coordinator, treasurer, and secretary selected by the members. Most of the *kelompok* members had previous experience with batik making as workers and/or middlewomen, but none had been an entrepreneur. A number of members were active in the PKK, Dharma Wanita, and other government-sponsored village activities. The Wukirsari group maintained a savings and loan scheme and conducted a monthly lottery among its members. Some women were reluctant to join the project because husbands objected that it would take time away from housework and other income-producing activities such as trading in semi-finished batik.

The *kelompok* was provided with training, equipment, raw materials, and advice on product design and marketing. The most important of these inputs were raw materials and training in the naphtol dyeing process. Cloth and dyestuffs, but not credit, were first given free and later on a subsidized basis. Mastery of the dyeing process allowed the members total control over production because they were no longer required to take semi-finished cloth to entrepreneurs in Imogiri and Yogyakarta for dyeing. At first, dyeing was done at the village headman's house under his wife's supervision. As members became more proficient, the *kelompok* split into five smaller production groups. Four of these groups were still active five years later.

The membership of the *kelompok* grew from the original 26 to 38 women who now employ 166 workers. Several of the original members are no longer active because they could not afford to spend the time away from home required by *kelompok* activities. One woman resettled elsewhere, and another lost interest after becoming a successful entrepreneur. Five of the 38 *kelompok* members became independent producers, one of whom is also the inactive entrepreneur. Each of these five women was the head of one of the production groups, served as an officer in the *kelompok,* and was previously established as a middlewoman. Three of the women had relatives in other areas with access to secure markets. A fourth combines subcontracting for a Jakarta designer with independent marketing. The fifth sells her work primarily to visitors.

The other *kelompok* members work as wage laborers for the more successful women or continue to depend mostly on their individual activities as middlewomen. They produce finished batik only when there is an order from the village headman's wife, the provincial coordinator, or another government official. Relationships between workers and middlewomen have changed very little with the adoption of their new role. Both entrepreneurs and middlepeople try to minimize labor costs by offering loans that recipients repay by selling their batik work at reduced prices.

Entrepreneurs are still new and working with rather small quantities of cloth. In general, they provide work to fewer artisans than in the past. In contrast, middlepeople are already long established and handle higher volumes.

Table 4.9 compares monthly income and expenses for middlewomen and entrepreneurs involved in the P2WIK-UNDP project in Wukirsari. Monthly income for nonproject batik workers in Wukirsari averaged Rp 7,942 in January 1985. Average monthly income for workers' households was Rp 51,055. Appendix 4B describes the situation of a batik worker in the hamlet of Giriloyo in the village of Wukirsari. Giriloyo has the highest concentration of batik makers, middlewomen, and project participants in the village. The higher-income households had a greater number of employed persons and one or more members employed in a comparatively high-paying job such as house building or public service. The majority of worker households were dependent on income from batik combined with subsistence agriculture or earnings from agricultural labor, and fell into the village's lower economic stratum.

When the project began, no finished batik was produced in Wukirsari. Productivity increased to support continuous production by four small groups, each of which had the capacity to turn out 20 hand-drawn medium- to high-quality *kain* per month. In addition to traditional garments, product differentiation included cloth for men's shirts, tablecloths, pillow covers, and scarves. Two of the working group members experimented with non-traditional colors.

Without the urban entrepreneur, women found the local market very limited, and they did not know how or where to market their finished batik. The program director and regional coordinator from the Department of Industry provided some assistance by arranging for the group's work to be displayed in exhibits and by bringing in buyers from Jakarta and official tour groups. *Kelompok* members were encouraged to accept orders from well-known urban entrepreneurs introduced to them by government representatives and to accept subcontract negotiations made on their behalf. These arrangements were not always as profitable as marketing their work on their own. For example, one of the most active subcontractors reported that it was difficult to find workers willing to do the detailed patterns sent by a well-known Jakarta designer. She often had to go to a neighboring village where rates were higher in order to get the work done. After expenses, her profit was only Rp 1,500 for a three-meter length. She made Rp 5,000 to 10,000 on work she markets herself. The *kelompok* members felt frustrated with their inability to develop secure markets. The regional coordinator told them their work would be more marketable if it were of higher quality, but some members consciously market through the group only those pieces that they cannot sell on their own.

Table 4.1 Division of Labor by Gender in Home-
and Factory-based Batik Production

Process	Home-based	Factory-based
Pattern design	F	M
Cutting cloth	F	F, M
Cloth preparation	F	(no longer done)
Drawing designs (*tulis* only)	F	F
Waxing (first, second, third)	F	F, M (*canting*)
		M (*cap*)
Dyeing (first, second)	F	M
Scraping	F	M
Boiling	F	M
Finishing	F	M
Sewing (nontraditional products)	—	F, M
Packaging	—	F

Source: Joseph (1987).

Table 4.2 Land Ownership among Batik Households (percentages)

	Landless	Up to 0.3 hectares	0.3–0.5 hectares	More than 0.5 hectares
Rural	60	31	2	4
Urban	92	4	—	4

Source: Joseph (1987).

Table 4.3 Mean Monthly Income (in Rp) from Batik Work, 1984

	Women	Men
Urban	17,417	46,500
Rural	12,760	17,000
Mean	15,088	31,750

Source: Joseph (1987).

Table 4.4 Age of Entry into Batik Industry (percentages)

Age	Women	Men
5–12	50	25
13–18	38	35
19–35	11	30
over 35	1	10
Total	100	100

Source: Joseph (1987).

Table 4.5   Batik Work as Percentage of Household Income

	25%	25–49%	50–74%	75–79%	100%
Rural households	17	24	22	5	32
Urban households	20	20	20	7	33
Total	19	22	21	6	33

Source: Joseph (1987).

Table 4.6   Workers per Household Engaged in Wage Labor (percentages)

	One Worker	Two Workers	Three or More Workers
Rural	4.9	43.9	51.2
Urban	—	93.3	6.7

Source: Joseph (1987).

Table 4.7   Workers per Household Engaged in Batik Industry (percentages)

	One Worker	Two Workers	Three or More Workers
Rural	43.9	29.3	26.8
Urban	66.7	33.3	—

Source: Joseph (1987).

Table 4.8   Occupations of Batik Household Members
Employed Outside the Industry (percentages)

	Rural	Urban
Agriculture	**45.6**	**9.1**
Farmer	17.1	—
Agricultural laborer	28.6	9.1
Manufacturing	**17.1**	**27.3**
Batik entrepreneur	5.7	—
Factory worker	—	27.3
Crafts worker	11.4	—
Service	**20.6**	**36.4**
Religion teacher	5.7	—
Nurse	—	—
Transit worker	2.9	—
Small trader	8.6	9.1
Seamstress/tailor	2.9	9.1
Driver	—	9.1
Informal	**17.2**	**27.3**
Pedicab driver	2.9	18.2
Skilled laborer	2.9	—
Unskilled laborer	11.4	9.1

Source: Joseph (1987).

Table 4.9 Monthly Balance Sheet for Middlewomen and
Entrepreneurs in Wukirsari (in Rp) P2WIK-UNDP Project

	Middlewomen	*Entrepreneurs*
Expenditures		
Cloth	3,619	89,879
Dyestuffs	—	23,785
Waxes	24,400	18,753
Wages	39,391	17,610
Firewood	—	3,659
Household expenses	35,980	75,014
Total expenditure	103,390	228,700
Total income	152,223	460,000
Net profit	48,834	231,300

Source: Joseph (1987).

Appendix 4A: The Batik *Tulis* Process

Batik tulis is made using a *canting,* a tool consisting of a copper well with one or more spouts affixed to a wooden handle. The well is dipped into a pot of hot wax. Then, by manipulating the angle of the instrument, a design is drawn in the fabric. *Batik tulis* is noted for the identical waxing of both sides of the cloth. Depending on the complexity of the design and the sizes of the *canting* used, the waxing processes take from a few days to more than six months to complete. When natural dyestuffs are used, production time is extended by several weeks. Because drying is most often done outside, bad weather can also lengthen the production time. In rural areas, dyeing ceases during the rainy season.

The traditional *batik tulis* production process consists of the following steps:

1. Sizing is removed from the cloth by soaking it in water overnight. The cloth is then beaten to ensure that all sizing has been removed.
2. After drying, the cloth is starched with a mixture of tapioca flour and water. The purpose of starching is to prevent the yarns from moving easily, to limit penetration of the hot wax, and to facilitate removal of the wax after dyeing.
3. After another drying, the starched sheets of cloth are folded and placed on a wooden mallet until smooth and uniform.
4. The first step in the waxing process is drawing the outline of the motifs and filling them in. This step is repeated on the reverse side.
5. Those parts of the cloth that are to remain white are then covered with wax on both sides of the cloth.

6. The cloth is ready for the first dyeing. It is placed in a tub of dissolved indigo paste so that all uncovered portions become dark blue.
7. Depending on the design, part of the previously applied wax is removed by scraping the cloth with a hand-held tool. Alternatively, the wax is boiled off.
8. The design elements to remain blue are covered with wax.
9. The cloth is submerged in a soga dye extract to obtain a golden to chocolate brown color. If traditional dyestuffs are used, up to twenty repetitions may be required to achieve the desired shade.
10. All of the remaining wax is removed by boiling the cloth in a copper kettle.

Contemporary batik makers usually streamline the production process: steps 1–3 are no longer practiced; dyestuffs are commercially prepared synthetics; and small areas may be painted with dye rather than waxing the entire piece and submerging in a dye bath, especially in pieces that feature as many as eight colors.

Appendix 4B: Life of a Wukirsari Batik Worker

Aminah is thirty years old and has completed six years of primary school. She has one daughter six months of age. Her first child, also a girl, died at age four and a half from fever. Aminah and her husband, thirty-five, support their household through a variety of economic activities. Her primary activity is making batik. She waxes two pieces of *sedang*-quality batik a month and sells these to one of the hamlet entrepreneurs, a project member, at a reduced price to repay the debt she incurred for her daughter's funeral. One week each month she assists the entrepreneur with dyeing and scraping. As a poor relation of the entrepreneur, Aminah benefits from newly created job opportunities, but she is not exempt from repaying debts in the traditional fashion.

Her husband farms the 0.2 hectares of rice land they recently inherited in addition to plowing the fields of other farmers. Aminah works with two hired laborers in their fields during planting and harvesting. In 1985, they harvested 1.5 quintals (150 kilograms) of rice, which they consumed themselves. They also grew mung and string beans. However, income from the sale of their surplus (Rp 7,000) was consumed by the cost of inputs for their failed peanut crop (Rp 10,000). Twice a month Aminah's husband sells firewood that he collects from the hillsides above the village. For each trip to the market in Imogiri, he brings home Rp 1,000.

Table 4B.1 shows the financial resources and the cash flow for Aminah's household. Average monthly household expenditures total Rp 18,700, almost all on food. Aminah and her family regularly contribute small sums to various village organizations such as the mosque fund and the village treasury. At weddings and funerals, they ordinarily give a modest Rp 1,500, and they buy new clothes only before Lebarn, the feast at the end of the fasting month. All of Aminah's household assets are in the traditional forms of gold, animals, and land. With the exception of the two cows that her husband uses in plowing and a small vegetable crop cultivated during the dry season, their assets are not income-producing. They do not own luxury goods such as radios, sewing machines, or vehicles.

Aminah handles all of the money in her household. The family's financial position worsened recently because of the expenditure required for the funeral arrangements of her elder daughter. She borrowed the money needed for feeding the mourners, a traditional Javanese custom, agreeing to repay it by selling her batik at a reduced price to the entrepreneur who made the loan. This led to a shortage of cash for daily necessities. The average monthly needs of Aminah's family surpass their income by Rp 3,650, an amount she borrows from her in-laws. If her situation deteriorates, she will be forced to sell assets.

Batik workers' mean monthly income in Wukirsari in January 1985 was Rp 7,942. Aminah's income would be much higher than the average were she not repaying a debt. Unlike the majority of women, she makes the more remunerative *sedang*-quality batik rather than the low-paying *kasar* quality. Her household is typical of the lower strata of batik workers, about

Figure 4A.1 Organization of Batik *Tulis* Production in Indonesia

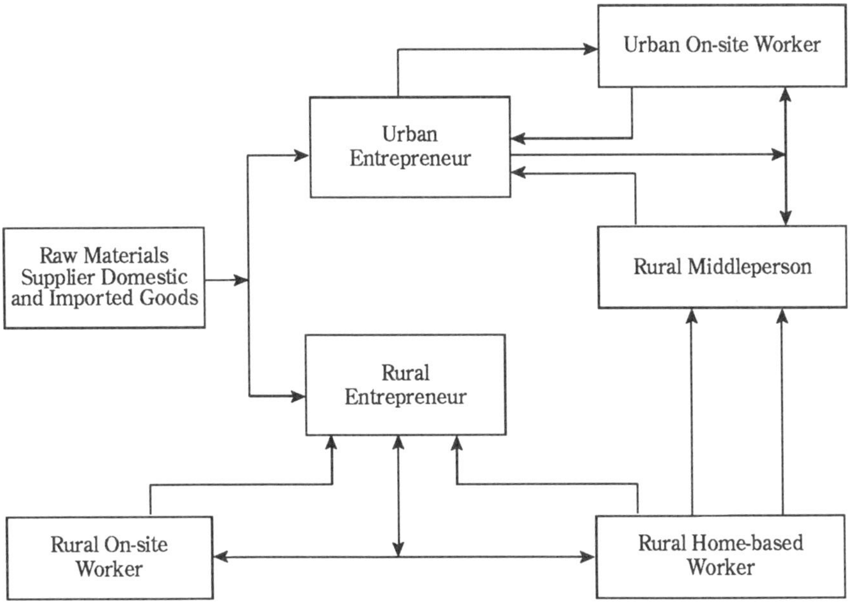

Source: Joseph (1987).

45 percent of the village households. Higher-income households have a greater number of employed members and one or more employed in a high-paying job (e.g., house building, public service).

Table 4B.1   Income, Expenditures, and Assets (in Rp)
in a Batik Worker's Household, 1985

	Value	*Frequency*
Income Source		
Wife's selling semi-finished batik to village entrepreneurs	2,500/piece	2/month
Wife's assisting entrepreneur with dyeing	250/day	7/month
Wife's selling chickens	2,000/head	3/year
Husband's selling firewood at the local market	1,000/day	2/month
Husband and wife's farming, sale of surplus mung and green beans	7,000/year	1/year
Husband's plowing	3,000/day	21/year
Average monthly income	15,083[a]	
Expenditures		
Rice	3,375	1/month
Food (other than rice)	10,000	1/month
Clothing	15,000	1/year
Travel to Yogyakarta	1,000	2/month
Gifts at ceremonies, rituals	1,500	5/year
PKK, mosque fund, village fund	100	4/month
Agricultural inputs and wages to laborers	13,000	1/year
Child's funeral	44,150	once
Average monthly expenditures (excluding funeral expenses)	18,733[a]	
Assets		
1 bamboo-walled house	200,000	
1 house plot, 0.1 hectares	300,000	
1 plot of irrigated rice land, 0.2 hectares	600,000	
10 grams gold jewelry	115,000	
2 cows	600,000	
2 goats	80,000	
7 chickens	14,000	
Total assets	1,909,000	

[a]Weighted average of amount by frequency.
Source: Joseph (1987).

Case 5

Philippines: The Aslong
Irrigation Project

Two Villagers

Lydia

In the early years of her marriage, Lydia did mostly housework. Once her children were born, her husband's tuberculosis diminished his earning capacity, requiring Lydia to earn an income outside the home. By late 1985, her husband was completely bedridden. After that, she and her two oldest children supported him and the other four children.

Nearly everything they could earn went toward food. The staples were rice and root crops, and neighbors gave them vegetables. They bought dried fish once in two weeks, but a regular nonfood item they had to buy was kerosene for their lamp. Occasionally Lydia was able to buy a little coffee. Medical costs took a heavy toll on their funds. Clothes they got secondhand.

Most of the family income was from paddy shares Lydia and her two oldest children could earn as laborers. They received one-tenth of the crop they harvested and threshed. Additional cash income was earned by weeding and transplanting for nearby landowners. From time to time Lydia's family kept poultry or a pig to earn extra cash.

Although Lydia's life was always hard, she encouraged her family not to be without hope. Her family's hut was on a knoll surrounded by rice fields. She valued their location because she could monitor the activities at the

This case was adapted for teaching by Leslie W. Tuttle and Catherine Overholt from Illo (1988).

surrounding farms and be the first to know when labor was needed. With irrigation in the area, a second rice crop was planted and more jobs for the landless resulted. The labor slump and food shortages that characterized the dry season without a rice crop disappeared.

Julia

Julia and her husband, Marciano, were sharecropping tenants working 1.8 hectares of land, of which not quite half was in rice cultivation serviced by the Aslong irrigation system. Irrigation had enabled them to grow a dry season crop for four of the past five years. One year a defective structure on the canal broke, depriving them of water.

Marciano joined the irrigators' association in order to be included in the system. From the beginning, he attended monthly assemblies and worked weekly on maintenance of the irrigation system. His participation increased when he was elected to the board of directors. He also served as the fee collector in his sector, receiving a 10 percent commission on the paddy that members paid as fees. Julia's involvement with the association included housing and feeding the government surveyors who worked in their sector and attending seminars in Marciano's place when he was unable to attend.

Aslong Region

High-yielding rice varieties were introduced into the Philippines in the 1960s. The early maturation of these varieties, combined with adequate irrigation, allowed farmers to grow a rice crop during the dry season. This was the first time they could produce two rice crops per year. The population of the Philippines increased at an annual rate of 2.7–3.0 percent during the 1960s and 1970s, and demand for food and jobs increased dramatically. Given that almost all of the country's arable land was already under production, the intensification of rice cultivation became the focus for meeting the country's expanding food needs.

Half of the country's irrigation systems are owned and operated by the government. The others are communal systems that owners use and operate. The government assists the communal systems through the National Irrigation Administration (NIA), which helped with the original construction of dams and other irrigation infrastructure.

In later years, the NIA recognized that among the factors hindering the operation of the irrigation systems was the lack of strong irrigators' organizations to manage them. Therefore, a government policy was issued for a participatory communal irrigation program aimed at building irrigators' associations. The Aslong project was one of two pilot projects meant to serve as a learning laboratory for the participatory approach.

The Aslong irrigation project was located in the Bicol region, the southernmost part of Luzon Island. The project villages surrounded a town called Libmanan in the province of Camarines Sur. Here the people were Bicolanos, one of the largest ethnic groups in the Philippines.

Traditionally, Bicol was a rice-growing area. Its tropical climate brought a rainy season from late May to December and a dry season from January to May. Until the 1960s, the farmers grew one rice crop in the wet season. After leaving their land fallow for a short period, they grew tubers and corn during the dry months. Twenty-five percent of the arable land was not under rice cultivation and was used for corn, squash, peppers, and other vegetables. Coconut and fruit trees grew in hilly areas. Vegetables and fruits were grown both for home consumption and as a source of additional income. With increased irrigation and the introduction of high-yielding rice varieties and insecticides, herbicides, and fertilizer, two rice crops with improved yields were possible. The increases were not sustained, however, during the 1970s because of various technical deficiencies and the lack of adequate management.

Until the early 1970s, vast areas of rice land in Aslong were owned by a small number of landlords who allowed large portions of their lands to be tilled by share tenants. The tenants usually kept 50–60 percent of their harvest, paying the rest to the landlord. Land reform initiatives instituted by the government during the 1970s aimed to improve the terms of share tenancy and provide cultivators with greater control over their produce. A certification of land transfer program was initiated to facilitate the purchase of land by those who worked it. In spite of these efforts, about one-third of the households in the Aslong project area still had no access to land. In 1985, share tenants still accounted for 30 percent of the water users along the Aslong system. The other users (in percentages) were as follows: lessees (27), owner/cultivators (10), other contracts (13). Average farm size was 1.8 hectares. This figure dropped steadily as a result of the division of land by the original owners among their heirs, the sale of lands for nonagricultural uses, and the land reform efforts.

In the project area, half of the households cultivate rice. The rest grow corn or tubers, look after coconut plantations, grow other cash crops, engage in trading, or work at wage labor. The income earners of a family usually engage in a variety of activities. New ventures are often tried, and frequent changes are made in search of better income. Most households also raise chickens, geese, ducks, and one or two pigs. Some have carabao, goats, or cattle.

In the Aslong region of the Philippines, the activities of women and men are not rigidly defined. Men usually assume greater responsibility for affairs outside the family. Farming decisions are made jointly by husbands and wives, and women contribute substantially to nearly all aspects of rice production. Men and women work in the fields together. Men undertake the land preparation for the rice paddy. Women predominate in the tasks of planting and transplanting. Male and female workers are paid equally for transplanting and weeding. They each earn a share (between one-tenth and one-eighth) of the gross paddy they harvest and thresh. Men earn twice the daily wage rate for other tasks when doing mechanized work. Women in landholding families are usually in charge of hiring and supervising contract labor required for weeding, transplanting, and harvesting the paddy. Fifty-six percent of wage laborers are female. In addition, women are primarily responsible for domestic production and household maintenance. Among female-headed households, women take on all the tasks usually relegated to men, although some women can afford to hire labor or have male relatives living close by who can help. Most, however, have preferred to do the work of preparing the land themselves.

Women in most households are responsible for purchasing all farm inputs and household necessities from the city market. They also market their own goods and run small stores or concessions. Although they are a minority in the market, women are not prohibited by custom from bringing their produce or products to market and conducting their own businesses.

Women control the liquid assets of households. Generally, the wife of the household is given the cash earnings of her husband and children to use for household expenses. Men rarely hand over all their earnings, reserving an average 10 percent for liquor, cigarettes, and cockfighting. Because women are responsible for making up any deficit in the household budget, most women engage in a range of small-scale enterprises or wage work in addition to their home production tasks. Informal cash loans are available to both men and women. Credit from rural banks is more accessible to men because banks require women (but not men) to secure their spouses' approval before applying for credit.

The division of labor among the project area families is illustrated in Table 5.1. Time allocations for these activities (postproject data) indicated that the average married woman spends 1.5 hours daily in market production and 8.9 hours in household production. The average married man spends 2 hours daily in market production work and 2.8 hours in household chores. For the landless, farm-related labor in these categories is work done for others in exchange for wages or goods.

Children in all classes assume chores starting at a very young age. Boys fetch water and run errands; girls help their mothers within the household. Many children leave elementary school to aid their parents in income-producing tasks. By the time they are twelve, they also may be hired as wage laborers in the rice fields. Teenage girls often leave home to become domestic servants in the city, sending home most of their earnings.

The immediate cash needs of the family often dominate over the best intentions to see children extend their education. Families display a range

Table 5.1 Division of Work among Household Members
in the Aslong Project Area by Gender and Age

Adult Workers	*Child Workers*
Predominantly female	
Raising of fowl/swine	Helping in the feeding of animals
Cultivation of kitchen gardens	Helping in keeping kitchen gardens
Transplanting/planting	Washing dishes
Weeding	Cleaning house/yard
Harvesting	Caring for younger siblings
Nonmechanized threshing	Helping in food preparation
Selection/preservation of seeds/	
planting materials	
Contacting buyers/hired workers	
Preparation of food	
Marketing for household	
Buying farm inputs/selling farm outputs	
Child care/training	
Care of sick household members	
Household laundry	
Predominantly male	
Land preparation	Bringing animals to pasture
Spraying chemicals/fertilizers	Gathering firewood
Seedbed preparation	Fetching water
Mechanized farm tasks	
Hauling/transporting farm goods	
Harvesting/husking of coconuts	
Drying of copra	
Repair of bunds and irrigation canals	
Repair of house	

Source: Illo (1988).

of attitudes about the amount of schooling necessary for boys and girls. Many argue that girls only need training to be housewives and conclude that more than a few years of school are a waste. Others recognize the greater range of earning opportunities made available through extended education. Many children may be prevented from continuing their educations for economic reasons, though income level is not the only factor that determines school attendance. Attitudes for and against continued education exist in each income group.

Most major family decisions involve a joint consultation between the man and woman. The majority of couples consult with each other on matters such as the acquisition, utilization, and disposal of resources. Under the Philippine Civil Code, lands acquired after marriage are conjugally owned. A husband's signature is required for a woman to sell her own or their joint property. Control of nonliquid resources, such as the raising and breeding of animals, usually falls to the partner most involved in their production.

Control over household earnings is described in Table 5.2.

Women's presence in public life is accepted in general, although their participation in community activities other than the marketplace is limited. Traditionally, they participate actively in civic and religious affairs. Wealthier women are more likely to be seen in public activities because they can afford the time away from household income-generation tasks. Most women are under constant pressure to engage in a range of small-scale enterprises or wage work in addition to their home production tasks. Although encouraged to attend meetings and cast votes, women are rarely elected to office or selected for leadership roles.

Table 5.2   Control over Types of Household Earnings

Type of Earnings and Person in Control[a]	Number of Households (n = 90)
Wage earnings of female members	
Women	34
Men	—
Joint	10
Wage earnings of male members	
Women	36
Men	7
Joint	27
Proceeds from sale of paddy	
Women	31
Men	5
Joint	3
Earnings from garden and other nonrice crops	
Women	28
Men	4
Joint	4
Earnings from livestock	
Women	31
Men	—
Joint	7
Earnings from poultry	
Women	29
Men	—
Joint	5
Earnings from trading	
Women	24
Men	—
Joint	7

[a]Not all categories are applicable to all households.
Source: Illo (1988).

Project Design and Implementation

The first Aslong irrigation system was built by farmers in the early 1900s. A medium-sized communal system of the gravity type, it consisted originally of two temporary dams constructed of coconut trunks, stones, bamboo, and soil. These were built along the Aslong River to divert water into a network of delivery canals. Because the monsoons repeatedly destroyed the dams, they required constant repair. The farmers along the system drew water for irrigation and maintained them as best they could.

The users of the Aslong system requested the assistance of the National Irrigation Administration (NIA) for the construction of a concrete dam and improvement of the irrigation canals. The NIA responded positively with the hope that Aslong would provide an opportunity to use its new participatory approach. Farmers would provide labor and materials in the construction phase and pay back a significant portion of the construction costs. The irrigators' group would own and operate the completed system.

The goals of the Aslong project were (1) to increase food production; (2) to raise family income and improve the quality of life; (3) to generate employment opportunities; and (4) to involve farmers in the design, construction, operation, and maintenance of the irrigation system for purposes of their becoming more capable of managing the system and repaying their construction loan. The government also hoped that the benefits from the project would reach not only the irrigation users but other households as well.

A prerequisite for government assistance was farmers' interest and willingness to work with the NIA in the participatory strategy. This strategy was meant to ensure the ongoing maintenance and management of the irrigation system. Farmers would provide labor and materials in the construction phase and repay a significant portion of the construction costs. Users were required to organize into an irrigators' association, the members of which were the heads of households of landowning and share tenant farmers whose fields could be irrigated by the system.

Two female community organizers spent nine months in the four villages before construction, first in conducting a socio-technical profile of the project area through interviews of male heads of households and later helping farmers organize and plan. The irrigators' association then negotiated with the NIA concerning design of the system. Finally, the participatory strategy required that the irrigators' association own, operate, and maintain the completed system.

The unit of participation chosen by project designers for this project when it started in the late 1970s was "head of household." Most households in the area had males as their heads; only a few female-headed households existed. Planners assumed that household heads would be able to speak for the entire household and that all family members would benefit from participation of their head in the project. When the irrigators' association was formed, men constituted 90 percent of the membership. When the project was implemented, the male farmers challenged the fact that only heads of households were eligible for formal participation in association meetings and other project activities. They frequently sent their wives as proxies to association meetings.

After the nine months of field work by the female NIA community organizers to develop the irrigators' association, construction started in 1979. A concrete dam was constructed upstream of the original dam. Labor for construction was recruited from potential users and landless wage laborers. The dam and canal structures were completed in September 1980. Repair of defective structures and installation of siphons and flumes ended early in 1982. The project included four villages: San Isidro in the upper half of the system and Bahay, Aslong, and Palangon in the lower half.

Construction of the dam, excavation and compacting of 17.2 kilometers of canals, and installation of canal structures and pipes generated 27,791 person-days of labor. Efforts were made to use labor-intensive technologies in order to maximize employment activities. Most of the labor was done by association members, though some female heads of households sent male proxies in their places. Association members had 21.7 percent of their daily wages deducted as part of the loan repayment program. Some landless men and other farmers were contracted by the association for some aspects of the construction work. Because labor of this kind was considered too heavy for women, they were not recruited for these jobs.

The irrigation system was turned over to farmers in June 1982. The total cost of the project was $81,557, of which $67,954 represented the association's loan. By early 1986, $1,636 had been repaid to the irrigation office. To help the association effectively operate the system and repay its loan, the NIA provided seminars in financial management, water management, and rice production. In crop year 1985–86, the system irrigated 227 hectares in the dry season and 231 in the wet season. This compared with 209 and 230 hectares, respectively, before NIA's assistance.

Project Impact

A study of project impact was conducted in 1985. Three research methods were used. The first was a community study that asked key informants to relate patterns of behavior concerning land use and contracts, production technologies, labor utilization, and access to development agencies and markets. Systems operation and maintenance problems were also discussed. A second research technique was used to record the life histories of six households as related by the women in them. The households reflected upper- and lower-system users and association members and nonmembers. These interviews focused on family histories, resources, sources of income, production arrangements, division of labor, community ties, and participation in irrigation activities.

The final research method was a household survey conducted to investigate the impact of the Aslong irrigation project on the different types of households. Ninety of the 287 households in the area were surveyed, representing upper and lower regions, members and nonmembers.

Agricultural Production

Table 5.3 indicates the overall number of hectares available for irrigated rice cultivation before and after the Aslong project. Dry season impact had the greatest cumulative effect. Because of changes in the irrigation patterns, structural breakdowns, and inadequate management, some of the areas experienced a decrease in irrigated area. Tables 5.4 and 5.5 provide the number of households that benefited from the Aslong system. Almost half (48 percent) of the households that were members of the irrigation project had not farmed rice before the project was implemented. The average size of the rice farms decreased from a little over 1.0 hectare in crop year 1978–79 to 0.9 hectare in 1985–86. Of the thirteen new families, five had moved to the area, and eight had acquired cultivation rights.

Table 5.3 Irrigated Area Estimates (in hectares) for the Aslong System by Crop Season, 1979 and 1985–86

Village/ Sector	1979		1985–86		Increase/ (Decrease)	
	Dry	Wet	Dry	Wet	Dry	Wet
San Isidro Sagop 1	53.8	35.1	50.5	50.2	(3.3)	15.1
San Isidro Sagop 2	56.5	56.5	60.5	60.5	4.0	4.0
Bahay[a]	—	—	15.4	13.3	15.4	13.3
Aslong	24.9	22.8	26.5	25.1	1.6	2.3
Palangon-1	56.4	56.4	41.4	41.0	(15.0)	(15.4)
Palangon-2	38.2	37.9	36.7	36.4	(1.5)	(1.5)
Total	229.8	208.7	231.0	226.5	1.2	17.8

[a]10–12 hectares of Bahay had been irrigated by the old Aslong system, but in 1979 poor upstream maintenance caused a stoppage in the water flow.
Source: Illo (1988).

Table 5.4   Number of Households Cultivating Irrigated
Rice Farms by Crop Season, Pre-1979 and 1985–86

Village/ Sector	Pre-1979		1985–86		Increase/ (Decrease)	
	Dry	Wet	Dry	Wet	Dry	Wet
San Isidro Sagop 1	54	33	53	53	(1)	20
San Isidro Sagop 2	2	55	55	61	61	6
Bahay	—	—	22	19	22	19
Aslong	24	24	26	25	2	1
Palangon-1	59	59	51	50	(8)	(1)
Palangon-2	34	34	33	33	(1)	(1)
Total	223	205	246	241	20	36

Source: Illo (1988).

Table 5.5   Distribution of Sample Rice Farming Households Based
on 1979 Cultivation, by Location and Beneficiary Category

Village/Beneficiary Category	Rice Farm in 1979 and 1985	Rice Farm Only in 1985	Total
San Isidro			
Direct beneficiary	16	17	33
Indirect beneficiary	8	—	8
Total	24	17	41
Palangon			
Direct beneficiary	10	7	17
Indirect beneficiary	3	2	5
Total	13	9	22
Overall			
Direct beneficiary	26	24	50
Indirect beneficiary	11	2	13
Total	37	26	63

Source: Illo (1988).

Paddy production increased in both upper and lower regions during the dry season, whereas only the upper region showed an increase during the wet season (Table 5.6). A reliable irrigation supply is most critical during the dry season. Therefore, only those nonmember households that irrigated their farms by impounding runoff or drainage water from the Aslong system realized yields as high as those of the association members.

Paddy production increases occurred without any complementary improvements in rice farm technology. Plowing and harrowing were done largely by carabaos. Tractors were used only where the mud was too deep for the animals. Although a small shift toward broadcasting seeds emerged as a result of increased labor costs, most crops were transplanted from seedbeds. Herbicides and insecticides were reportedly used in moderation throughout this period, and the high cost of fertilizer in 1985 reduced its usage. The only significant technological change between 1979 and 1985 was the increasing use of mechanical threshers. In light of these factors, farmers attributed better paddy production per hectare in 1985 to the improved irrigation service.

Increases in paddy production between 1979 and 1985 are estimated at 117 tons during the wet season and 248 tons during the dry season, totaling an increase of 365 tons per crop year. This represents a simple annual rate of increase of 9 percent. Compared with the concurrent population growth rate of 2.7 percent, the food production capacity engendered by improvements in the Aslong system was significant.

Employment and Income

The results of the household survey suggest that farm employment increased, both within families and for hired labor in construction and rice cultivation, as a result of this project. Although no preproject statistics are available for comparison, the responses to the household surveys indicated that the households felt the amount of labor involved per hectare in field operations was the same in 1985 as before the irrigation project was implemented. The expansion of the total area cultivated increased the total person-days of farm employment by about 190 person-days in the wet season and 2,619 person days during the dry season, or 2,809 per year. Of these jobs, 56 percent were filled by hired labor.

The daily wage rate doubled outside the project area during the project construction and implementation period and changed hiring patterns within the project area. Family labor substituted for paid laborers whenever possible. (Table 5.7 shows labor allocations.) Although overall the amount of labor hired for construction and rice cultivation increased as a result of the irrigation project, the anticipated increase was mitigated because of the rise in wage rates. Family substitution occurred for transplanting and weeding (dry season). Women accounted for 70–80 percent of all hired transplanters. The increased use of mechanical threshers also reduced the expected increases in wage labor hired.

Disturbances in the national economy canceled out the positive gains that would have been realized by the increased income generated by the irrigation project. The effects of the project cushioned households slightly from the full effects of national trends. During the period 1979–85, the price of consumer goods rose rapidly. Agricultural wages also rose, but not as quickly as the cost of consumer goods. Similarly, there was a disproportionately greater increase in the price of farm inputs as compared with the farm gate price of paddy. The average annual family income in the Aslong project area rose by 15 percent between 1980 and 1985, but prices rose at an average annual rate of 40 percent. Declines in real household income were offset by loans and reduced expenses. Purchased food items, clothes, and education were the expense items most frequently reduced. The landless reduced their already limited expenses even more. Women in all groups came under increasing pressure to secure other economic resources (Table 5.8) to meet family needs (Table 5.9).

Distribution of income in the project area varied dramatically. Estimates of average annual household incomes in San Isidro for the upper half of the system were more than double those of the lower half. However, these estimates include nonfarming households whose earnings are much higher than farm incomes. Farming households that were association members benefited directly from the project and had much higher household earnings than nonmembers. Nonmembers had higher wage earnings. A significant portion of earnings for all households came from the female activities of raising animals and trading.

Table 5.6   Comparative Rice Yields (ton/hectare) by Season and Location, Crop Years 1979–80 and 1985–86

Crop Year/Location	Wet Season	Dry Season
1979–80		
Upper half	n.d.	n.d.
Lower half	n.d.	n.d.
Overall	1.4	1.2
1985–86		
Upper half	2.1	2.4
Lower half	1.4	1.8
Overall	1.9	2.2

Note: The yield data for 1979–80 were based on Table 11 in Dozina and Early (1981); those for 1985–86 were computed based on the study's household survey data; n.d. = no data.
Source: Illo (1988).

Table 5.7 Average Labor Requirements (person-days per hectare) of Rice Farms, Crop Year 1985–86

Activity/ Type of Labor	Wet Season			Dry Season		
	Female	Male	Total	Female	Male	Total
Land preparation						
Hired	—	10.3	10.3	—	8.8	8.8
Family	—	25.2	25.2	—	23.3	23.3
Subtotal	—	35.5	35.5	—	32.1	32.1
Planting/ transplanting						
Hired	19.3	4.9	24.2	20.1	7.5	27.6
Family	2.5	3.9	6.4	2.9	4.0	6.9
Subtotal	21.8	8.8	30.6	23.0	11.5	34.5
Weeding						
Hired	7.6	5.7	13.3	8.4	4.6	13.0
Family	7.2	10.1	17.3	8.7	9.6	18.3
Subtotal	14.8	15.8	30.6	17.1	14.2	31.3
Harvesting/threshing						
Hired	19.0	13.2	32.2	17.1	15.9	33.0
Family	5.0	6.3	11.3	0.9	2.2	3.1
Subtotal	24.0	19.5	43.5	18.0	18.1	36.1
Other field activities						
Hired[a]	2.4	6.4	8.8	2.7	9.7	12.4
Family[b]	—	5.2	5.2	0.1	4.6	4.7
Subtotal	2.4	11.6	14.0	3.8	14.3	17.1
Labor supervision						
Hired	—	—	—	—	—	—
Family	6.2	4.2	10.4	5.6	2.9	8.5
Subtotal	6.2	4.2	10.4	5.6	2.9	8.5
All rice farming operations						
Hired	48.3	40.5	88.8	48.3	46.5	94.8
Family	20.9	54.9	75.8	18.2	46.6	64.8
Total	69.2	95.4	164.6	66.5	93.1	159.6

[a]Includes hauling and postthreshing activities.
[b]Includes activities such as applying fertilizers and pesticides.
Source: Illo (1988).

Table 5.8   Comparative Average Annual Household Earnings (pesos) by Source, Location of Farm, and Beneficiary Category

	Location		Category of Household			
Source of Income	Upper Half	Lower Half	Direct	Indirect Farming	Indirect Landless	Overall
Own enterprise						
Rice	1,772	1,300	2,404	1,272	—	1,615
Other crops	740	776	921	1,007	85	752
Animal care	1,042	342	403	884	1,795	809
Trading	1,949	321	1,348	240	2,318	1,406
Others	23	137	94	33	6	61
Subtotal	5,526	2,876	5,170	3,436	4,204	4,643
Wage employment of members[a]						
Female	1,431	381	764	2,323	543	1,081
Male	2,973	1,717	2,031	3,474	2,915	2,554
Subtotal	4,404	2,098	2,795	5,797	3,458	3,635
Total Income	9,930	4,974	7,965	9,233	7,662	8,278
Remittances from family members						
Female	216	160	300	78	60	197
Male	628	239	543	136	782	498
Subtotal	844	399	843	214	842	696
Earnings from all sources	10,774	5,373	8,808	9,447	8,504	8,974

[a]The difference between male and female wage earnings resulted primarily from the longer average hours spent by men than women on wage jobs.
Source: Illo (1988).

Participation

Table 5.10 indicates how user families assessed the participation of male and female members in project activities. The farming women interviewed expressed different attitudes toward participating in the project, ranging from reticence to engage in public affairs to eagerness to have a role for themselves. The average female household member spends twice as much time working every day as her husband.

Women constituted about 10 percent of the association membership, which in early 1983 totaled 165. A significant number of the women attending meetings were members, but many of them came as representatives of male association members. At least 25 percent of the sampled households regularly sent proxies; at some point, all used the proxy system. The community organizers who aimed to build farmers' commitment to the project by getting them engaged in project activities initially objected to the practice of sending proxies to meetings and other activities. They raised this issue several times, but several male leaders defended the members' strategy of sending their spouses to activities that the members could not attend. The leaders argued that the women, who were the usual proxies, were as involved in the cultivation of their farms as their husbands. The women had considerable power over household funds, and collection of irrigation fees and membership dues would be facilitated if the women were present during discussions of members' financial obligations to the association. Over time, the proxy issue was partly resolved with the proxies (whether male or female) being tolerated during meetings, but not allowed to vote on issues.

The landless were not invited to participate in the irrigation project activities except as wage laborers.

Table 5.9   Mean Annual Family Expenses (pesos) by Type of Expense, Location of Household, and Beneficiary Category

| | Location | | | Category of Household | | |
Source of Income	Upper Half	Lower Half	Direct	Indirect Farming	Indirect Landless	Overall
Food	10,058	8,762	10,320	11,718	5,986	9,626
Own produce[a]	4,770	4,867	6,146	5,637	800	4,802
Purchased	5,288	3,895	4,174	6,081	5,186	4,824
Clothes	682	366	471	882	496	574
Education	1,322	921	1,041	1,297	512	1,187
Medical care	455	249	399	603	114	386
Recreation	920	805	952	869	708	882
Cigarettes	602	636	694	592	415	614
Liquor/gambling	212	99	149	217	200	174
Movies	106	70	109	60	93	94
Total expenses	13,437	11,103	13,183	15,369	7,816	12,655
Total earnings	10,774	5,373	8,808	9,447	8,504	8,974
Surplus (Deficit)	(2,663)	(5,730)	(4,375)	(5,922)	687	(3,681)

[a]Market value equivalent of food produced by the household.
Source: Illo (1988).

Table 5.10   Male and Female Participation in Aslong Project Activities

Phase and Activity	Male	Female
Preconstruction:		
Developing the irrigators' association (IA)	Male leaders formed the committees to prepare the bylaws, register the IA with the Securities and Exchange Commission, apply for water permit, and recruit members. Male members dominated the meetings.	Women, either as members of the IA or as proxies of their spouses, attended general assemblies as well as sectoral meetings convened to discuss the bylaws.
Designing system facilities, undertaking surveys and field inspections to finalize the system design, and negotiating for rights of way (ROW)	Male farmers composed the bodies created to oversee or coordinate farmers' involvement in system planning activities. Men also joined surveys and assisted the NIA technical staff in paddy mapping. Male leaders undertook ROW negotiations.	A few female farmers joined NIA engineers and male members in field inspections to check the feasibility of suggested irrigation facilities and structures. Women attended the sessions to discuss system design. IA negotiators met with the men and their wives to secure ROW donations for canals or to decide on ROW payments for crop damages.
Construction:		
Preparation for farmers' participation in construction	Male leaders composed the majority of those who attended meetings with NIA engineers to discuss construction agreements and conditions. With one exception, the construction committees were composed exclusively of men.	A few female farmers and wives of male members joined NIA-IA discussions concerning system construction. A woman was named to chair the committee to monitor quality and quantity of construction material deliveries.
Construction	Male IA members served as contractors and construction workers.	Female members sent male proxies when IA mobilized its members to contribute labor as equity in the project.

Phase and Activity	Male	Female
Monitoring costs, materials, and farmers' contributions in the project	Committees formed to perform these functions, except for that on quality and quantity control, were composed of men.	Female head of committee on quality and quantity control discharged committee responsibilities almost single-handedly. Some women went to meetings where project costs and construction issues were discussed.
Contributions to the association's equity in the project	Farmers' contributions (of voluntary labor in surveys and in construction) came from male members and male representatives of female members. ROW donations came from female and male landowners.	Female members usually sent an adult member of their household as proxy in equity-generating activities. At least one female member paid the cash equivalent of the equity contribution.

Operation and maintenance (O&M):

Organizational restructuring prior to O&M	The IA leadership continued to be all-male except in 1981–82 when a woman served as IA treasurer.	In 1981–82, a woman was elected IA treasurer, and two women served as sector officers.
System management	Operations manager and O&M staff were generally male.	In 1981–82, there were two females on the O&M staff: the IA treasurer and a sector collector.
System maintenance	Initiators of and participants in group system maintenance and individual canal cleaning were usually male. Water tenders were male, too.	The female treasurer organized one maintenance effort and joined several others. She and the female treasurer collected fines from nonparticipants and used that money to buy snacks for system maintenance workers. Female members often sent male proxies to system maintenance group work.

Phase and Activity	Male	Female
Water Distribution	Scheduling of water distribution was the responsibility of O&M staff. Male and female members could draw water from the system by informing O&M officials.	Like male members, female members could draw water from the system by informing their sector water-tender.
Fee collection/financial management	In 1981–82, fee collection was a function of elected collectors/treasurers; in 1983–86, the collectors, concurrently sector representatives to the board of directors, were all men.	A woman was elected sector collector in 1981; subsequently, collectors were all men. Fee collections were remitted to the female treasurer in 1981–82; she was replaced by a man in 1983.

Note: The data for the preconstruction and construction phases were taken from Illo, de los Reyes, and Felix (1984); those for the O&M stage were taken from Illo and Volante (1984) and Illo (1985).
Source: Illo (1988).

Case 6

Thailand: The Saraburi
Dairy Farming Project

IN 1984, A PROJECT was begun to encourage dairy farming among women in the Muek Lek land reform area in the Saraburi Province of central Thailand. The project was the result of cooperation by a number of different institutions, including the Svita Foundation (a private, nonprofit organization that promotes small-enterprise development in Thailand), the Bangkok Bank (Thailand's largest commercial bank), the Thai Institute of Scientific and Technical Research (TISTR), and the Saraburi provincial administration. Three years later, the project operated in five villages and involved eighty-two families.

Muek Lek Land Reform Area and People

Located in the central province of Saraburi, about 250 kilometers northwest of Bangkok, the Muek Lek land reform area (LRA) was formerly government-owned reserve forest land. In 1979, a land reform program alloted plots of fifty *rai* (eight hectares) to each family living in the area and distributed the remaining land among landless agricultural laborers. Some families were able to get larger parcels of land by registering contiguous plots of fifty *rai* under the names of several family members.

Somchit and her family were typical of the area. She and her husband grew mostly maize and soybean on their thirty *rai* (4.8 hectares). Their land, as all land in the LRA, was owned by the government, but they had inheritable usufruct rights. Their four children all lived at home. The youngest, a boy four years old, was not yet in school. The two girls, ages

This case was adapted for teaching by Mary B. Anderson from Rao (1990).

eight and ten, both attended the village school, and the eldest, a boy seventeen, worked on the farm with his father and mother. In the dry season, he was usually able to find wage employment on irrigated farms in the southwest region of the province.

Somchit's land was in the somewhat hilly areas where soils were poor. She grew mostly maize, sorghum, mungbean, and soybean. Some of her neighbors also grew fruit trees; others raised chili, castor bean, and sugarcane. In the lowlands, a few neighbors planted rice in the poorly drained clay soils. Of all agricultural land in Muek Lek, 82 percent was devoted to maize production; rice growing accounted for less than 1 percent. The families who grew rice used it for their own consumption, whereas maize was grown mostly as a cash crop. Both the hilly and the lowlands areas relied solely on rain; there was no irrigation in this part of the province.

Somchit's family planted two maize crops per year. The main crop was planted in April, just before the rainy season that began in May and ended in October. Somchit's husband prepared the land in March. In some years, he was able to hire a tractor from one of the few men in the area who had raised enough capital to make the initial purchase investment. When he could not afford the tractors, he hired oxen from his neighbors who owned them. The men who owned oxen used them, first, for plowing their own land, but when that was complete, they were willing to rent them to other farmers. For the tractors, Somchit's husband paid about 18,200 baht (Bt), but the oxen rental was much less.

When the soil was plowed, Somchit would plant the seed and, with her husband and elder son, weed the crop for three or four weeks after planting. They never used either chemical fertilizers or pesticides because they could not afford them.

Everyone in the family worked together to harvest the crop in July. Under normal rains, they usually harvested about 2,100 kilograms per hectare. When the crop was good, they would often hire some labor to help with the harvest or work out a system of exchange labor with their neighbors.

As soon as the harvest was complete, Somchit's husband prepared the land for the second crop. Somchit again did the planting, though if for some reason it had to be done quickly, her husband and son helped. Weeding was usually only necessary once on this crop. Harvest would occur during November or early December. Because rains were lighter in this season, the yield of the second crop averaged only 1,500 kilograms per hectare. From November to February, the weather was quite cool, so no crop production was possible. It turned hot again in the premonsoon from February to April. Eighty-five percent of all rainfall was between May and October.

The two harvest seasons were also the seasons of household surplus income. A local merchant would come to the farm to purchase whatever

Somchit and her husband were willing to sell. He also did the milling of the maize with a portable milling machine, charging about Bt 2,000 for this service. Most farm families relied on merchants such as this one to purchase, process, and transport their crops. About 98 percent of maize produce was sold to these merchants, with farmers keeping the rest as seed for the next season. In an average year, Somchit's family received Bt 30,720 for their maize crop.

Mungbean and soybean, each accounting for about 10 percent of cultivated land, were also grown in two crop seasons, coinciding with those for maize. Tasks of land preparation, planting, weeding, and harvesting were carried out as for maize, and local merchants purchased these crops at the farm and carried out postharvest operations.

In most households in the area, it was the wife's responsibility to manage the household finances. Somchit usually had to use some of the harvest income to pay off the local merchants from whom she borrowed to cover expenses during the slack period. The merchants advanced her credit and charged 20 percent interest. Her net family income (and that of 70 percent of households in Muek Lek) averaged about Bt 10,000 per year. Thirty-five percent of her neighbors earned less than Bt 6,000 annually. Most years, Somchit could just cover household expenses, but during the three years 1982–1985 when there was drought, she fell behind and only managed to keep going through borrowing.

Somchit also did the other household work. She cleaned, prepared food, and did the laundry. Together, she and her husband cared for their youngest son while he was with them in the fields, but Somchit knew that she was really responsible for his needs and safety.

The two-room house, which her husband had built with the help of friends, was built up on stilts, as are most houses in this area of Thailand. The family kept a few animals in the area under the house. Somchit was responsible for feeding these chickens and two pigs, and she enjoyed the extra income she was able to earn from selling surplus eggs and, occasionally, a pig. Before the drought, Somchit's husband had hoped to be able to buy a pair of oxen to add to the family income as well.

Life was difficult for Somchit, but she knew that her family was better off than 10 percent of households in the area who had fewer than ten *rai* to farm.

History of Thai Dairy Industry

Milk consumption has not been traditional among the Thai people. Men traditionally raised cattle for draft use, beef, and manure rather than for dairy purposes. During the 1950s, however, Indian settlers around Ayutthaya (eighty kilometers north of Bangkok) began dairy farming. They sold their fresh milk to consumers in Bangkok. The government of

Thailand established a milk authority to promote milk production and consumption, but the imported milk products that were lower priced and better quality than domestic ones soon undermined domestic milk production. In the early 1960s, the governments of Denmark and West Germany began to assist the Thai government in dairy farming by establishing large-scale model dairy farms in Muek Lek and Chiang Mai. By 1972, there were eight milk processing factories producing pasteurized fresh milk and recombined milk in Thailand.

Between 1972 and 1982, the demand for milk grew at a rate of 25 percent per year. The increase resulted from a growing realization among the people that milk had high nutritional value and that producing it could increase family incomes. In addition, the government undertook a number of policies to promote milk production and consumption.

In the Fourth Development Plan (1975–1982), dairy farming was promoted through (a) the provision of long-term credit for dairy farming; (b) veterinary services, including artificial insemination and immunization of cattle against contagious diseases; (c) guaranteed prices for raw milk; and (d) importation of several thousand Sahiwal and Friesian heifers from New Zealand and Australia. The Fifth Development Plan (1982–1986) continued this trend, setting ambitious targets for raw milk production.

By 1983, the number of processing factories had risen to eleven. However, these factories still relied heavily on imported milk products that they combined with local raw milk. The availability of cheap surplus milk from European Economic Community (EEC) countries in 1983 caused a sudden increase in such imports.

In 1983, two legislative acts were enacted to promote local production and to limit imports of milk. The first, introduced by the Ministry of Industry, required producers of pasteurized or UHT (ultrahigh-temperature) milk to use a ratio of one to one raw fresh milk with recombined milk. The second, enacted by the Ministry of Commerce, involved the institution of a system of permits required for importing milk. Imports were allowed provided one kilogram of fresh milk was purchased for every one kilogram of imported powder (equivalent to eight kilograms of liquid milk). In 1984, a regulation was passed increasing the requirement for private factories making UHT milk to purchase ten units of local milk for each unit of imported powder. The requirement was again raised in 1985 to twenty units of local milk per single unit of imported powder.

From 114 dairy farmers with 3,450 cows in 1962, the dairy industry expanded to 4,000 farmers with 24,000 cows by 1986. Still, local production of milk lagged behind consumption, meeting only 10 percent of total demand. However, the Ministry of Agriculture and Cooperatives and the Ministry of Industry projected that after 1987 there would be a surplus of domestically produced fresh milk. They realized that new dairy products would need to be developed to absorb this surplus.

Muek Lek Dairy Project

In early 1984, the Thai Institute of Scientific and Technical Research (TISTR) was involved in a study of a large rural development project in a number of sites in Saraburi Province. TISTR's goal was to identify agricultural technologies that would enhance productivity and thus augment the incomes of local farmers. The executive director of SVITA, a nonprofit private organization concerned with small enterprise, was an adviser to TISTR, and she joined the TISTR team to Saraburi to explore opportunities for project activities that would improve farmers' lives.

The team visited various development sites with the Muek Lek land reform officer. One site they visited was that of the ongoing Thai government/Danish dairy project begun in the 1960s. The project was experiencing a number of difficulties, including low yields from the crossbreeds of European and local cattle and the lack of infrastructure, such as all-weather roads to connect farms with the milk processing plant thirty kilometers away.

Over several months, the team, working with the land reform officer, considered a range of options for promoting income generation among the Muek Lek farmers. They returned to the LRA to discuss their ideas with villagers on several occasions. Early on, the villagers formed an informal working group to consider the project options suggested to them by the TISTR team. In the beginning, this group had only one woman involved, but SVITA encouraged other women to join, and over time a number of them did. In spite of the problems the dairy project was encountering, everyone agreed that dairy farming represented a viable option for improving the livelihoods of Muek Lek farmers. Furthermore, there was strong interest in getting women involved in dairy farming because the cattle would require special feed and thus would not need to be taken out to graze. Women could fit the work with these cattle into their other work around the household.

With an associate, SVITA's director visited several small dairy projects sponsored by other nongovernmental organizations (NGOs) in Thailand. She and her associate conducted a feasibility study to determine the minimum level of production inputs necessary to make dairying profitable for a family in Muek Lek. They found that project feasibility rested on the acquisition of imported cows that yield higher quantities of milk than any of the local or crossbred varieties then in use. However, such imported cows were expensive, and capital was a problem. Efforts by the land reform officer and others to raise investment capital from the nationalized Bank for Agriculture and Cooperatives and the Bangkok Bank repeatedly failed.

Finding the Capital

A confluence of luck and entrepreneurial effort resulted in capital for the project. A senior vice president of the Bangkok Bank who was handling transactions for the Ministry of Agriculture to import cows called SVITA's director. She asked if SVITA would be interested in starting a dairy project. The director told her of SVITA's hopes for Muek Lek and the problems with raising the investment capital.

The two women devised a plan for raising capital by using the services of an international agency, Women's World Banking (WWB). WWB, formed during the 1975 United Nations Conference on Women, is an organization committed to providing access to credit and financial services for women in their local economies. Legally, both women and men had access to credit in Thailand. However, the major source of rural credit was the Bank for Agriculture and Cooperatives, and its rules stipulated that only "heads of households" were eligible for loans. This meant that almost all loans were made to men.

WWB had established a system for providing loan guarantees to lending institutions within a country when those institutions made loans to women. WWB guarantees limited the risk of institutions willing to lend to women. The Thai women approached WWB and received a Bt 5 million commitment for a three-year period. Thai NGOs set up a local WWB affiliate, Friends of Women's World Banking–Thailand (FWWBT). Three Thai NGOs pooled their capital and deposited Bt 750,000 in the Bangkok Bank as their portion of guarantee funds for credit to Muek Lek women. For each loan, WWB guaranteed 50 percent of the principal amount, FWWBT guaranteed 25 percent, and the bank bore the remaining risk. The loans were to be made exclusively to women, reflecting both the intentions of SVITA in starting this effort and the priorities of WWB.

The Bangkok Bank was at first reluctant to enter this new lending field, but the pooling of WWB and NGO funds greatly reduced its risk. In addition, the bank had been having difficulty meeting a legal requirement on its lending portfolio—namely, that 11 to 13 percent of its credit lending be to rural enterprises. Thus, the bank conducted its own feasibility study of the Muek Lek dairy scheme, basing the analysis on the importation of high-yielding cows. Realizing that SVITA was committed to providing ongoing supervision and technical assistance to the farmers who became involved in the scheme, the bank agreed to match the total WWB/ FWWBT deposit with its own funds and to make loans available to women recommended by the NGOs. For every baht deposited into this account, the bank agreed to make two bahts available for lending.

Project Design

SVITA began to conduct meetings with villagers in Muek Lek to discuss the dairy project. Many families wanted to participate, and eighty-five families applied for loans. The Bangkok Bank approved eighty-two of these applications. Women were the principal borrowers, with their husbands as cosigners (reversing the usual pattern in Thailand).

SVITA imported five hundred pregnant dairy cows from New Zealand. Each cow cost Bt 25,000 (U.S. $1,000). The project stipulated the following land/cattle ratio.

A woman holding:	Could buy:	With a loan of:
10–20 rai	up to 4 cows	Bt 158,000
21–30 rai	up to 5 cows	Bt 193,000
31–50 rai	up to 6 cows	Bt 229,000

The loans, higher than the per cow purchase costs, covered other start-up costs. These included electric fencing, barns, milking machines, water wells, and costs incurred during a two-month quarantine period as the cows were brought into the country. Loans were made at 13 percent annual interest (one percentage point below the going commercial rate). Repayment was scheduled over an eight-year period, with a twelve-month grace period. The monthly repayment amount of principal plus interest could not exceed 30 percent of a borrower-family's monthly income. The women borrowers were solely responsible for the financial management of the enterprise, though other family members were to be involved in raising and caring for the cattle.

Many people became involved in helping organize other necessary inputs. When the project began, there was no agricultural insurance in Thailand. With the Bangkok Bank's intervention, the Bangkok Insurance Company agreed to issue cattle insurance at the rate of Bt 800 per cow per year. Of the first importation of cows, twenty-three died from foot-and-mouth disease. The insurance covered 75 percent of the costs of replacement; the borrower bore the remaining loss. Most families who lost a cow immediately bought another in order to generate the income to pay back this loss on the loan.

In Muek Lek, the Dairy Farming Promotion Organization (DFPO) had begun with the start-up of the 1960s Danish project. This organization had held training courses in animal husbandry for local farmers several times each year. SVITA persuaded DFPO to hold a series of special training sessions for the Saraburi dairy farmers. These were arranged to coincide with the slack farming season. Courses lasted for one month and were held at the training facility. One member from each borrower-family was required to attend, and 70 percent of those who took the course were women. The provincial administration covered the costs of these courses.

The land reform officer coordinated the input of various services at the provincial level. The provincial veterinary office provided free general veterinary services to the farmers, except that farmers had to pay Bt 150 for semen from imported cows for artificial insemination (AI). It often re-

quired two or three AI attempts before a cow was successfully impreg-
nated, but if efforts were successful, the farmers could sell a male calf for
Bt 200 and a female calf for Bt 5,000. In the first year of the project, SVITA
arranged for the veterinarians to visit the borrowers' farms so that they
could teach the farmers while treating problems at the site. SVITA paid the
veterinarians for these extra services, which were provided on weekends
when they were off duty.

Because the New Zealand cows required an enriched feed to continue
to produce high yields, the provincial administration provided a Bt 200,000
grant for construction and purchase of necessary equipment for a feed mill
in 1984. SVITA provided a Bt 100,000 loan from its business development
fund to purchase a truck and establish a revolving loan fund.

All the borrowers became members of the feed mill, which they ran on
a cooperative basis. They elected a committee of ten farmers each year to
oversee general management, quality control, and money collection. Although the women were the borrowers, they usually elected men to these
positions because they preferred not to be involved in this aspect of the
dairy management.

A hired manager and manager's assistant handled day-to-day operations. They had two hired hands to grind and mix the feed. The manager
felt that the income benefits from the feed mill should be spread among
the local population, so she arranged to buy certain feed components,
such as maize, from local small farmers who did not own dairy cattle.
Other components for the feed were bought from a district town twenty
kilometers from Muek Lek. Farmers bought feed for their cows on credit
two times each month. The average cost per cow for enriched feed was Bt
550 per month.

The SVITA loan was repaid in 1987 from profits, and the feed mill then
collected Bt 500 from each borrower to replenish the revolving loan fund.
But the success of the mill was such that it began paying a dividend to its
members in the second year of operation. The total annual net profit of the
mill averaged between Bt 10,000 and Bt 15,000.

The Thai-Danish milk processing plant agreed to buy milk from the
FWWBT-assisted dairy farmers at the standard rate of Bt 6.50 per kilogram. Transportation of the milk to this processing plant was a problem
for many farmers; some lived as far as 50 kilometers away. Few of the borrowers owned trucks themselves, and the roads connecting the farms to
main provincial highways were bad or nonexistent. However, some Muek
Lek families did own trucks, and they saw this as an opportunity to make a
good profit. They agreed to transport the milk, but at very high prices.
SVITA intervened and worked with the dairy farmers to help them consider their alternatives, including using the feed mill truck or taking out an

additional loan to buy a new truck. When the local truck owners saw they could be underbid, they lowered their price to a reasonable rate, and ultimately they were hired by the farmers to transport the milk.

Later, SVITA persuaded the Thai-Danish plant to set up a milk collection center in the heart of Muek Lek and to establish twice-daily pickups in their refrigerated trucks. Women then only had to hire transportation to the collection center; the cost averaged between Bt 100 to Bt 300 per month, depending on the distance. SVITA also successfully lobbied for a public works scheme to construct roads linking the dairy project villages with the collection center and the milk processing plant.

The Thai-Danish milk processing plant also was responsible for arranging for the loan repayments of each farmer. The plant bought the milk from the farmers, totaling the amount it owed each month. Keeping separate accounts for each farmer, it deducted from the total owed (1) the amount owed the feed mill for the monthly consumption of feed, and (2) the monthly installment owed the bank. These payments were made directly by the processing plant management to the mill and to the bank, an arrangement that saved the borrowers the difficulty of traveling fifty kilometers each month to the nearest bank branch to make their payments. The remainder from the milk sales, if there was any, was paid directly to the dairy farmers.

Somchit's Decision

Somchit thought she wanted to become a dairy farmer. Her neighbor, Tipawan, had borrowed Bt 193,000 when the project first began and bought five cows, but almost immediately, one of the cows had died and two others became ill. Tipawan had been quite upset, and Somchit had decided to wait and see what happened before applying for a loan of her own.

Now it seemed Tipawan was doing very well, and Somchit thought that the arrangements for selling milk were running smoothly. She sat down to study some information (Tables 6.1 through 6.5) to figure out what size loan she would want and how much she could earn. She tried to anticipate any problems that would arise.

Table 6.1   Annual Average Farm Income (Bt) in Muek Lek LRA, 1987

Activity	Income	Expenses	Net Income
Maize Farming	30,720	20,224	10,496
Dairy Farming	95,730	58,651	37,079

Source: Rao (1990).

Table 6.2   Annual Average Net Income (Bt) per
Agricultural Household in Thailand, 1986

Northeast	18,666
North	28,770
South	31,638
East	53,778
West	49,986
Average	36,567

Source: Royal Thai Government, 1986.

Table 6.3   Average Household Income (Bt) by Source
in a Village Typical of Muek Lek LRA

Month	Source of Income (net)				
	Farm	Nonfarm	Wage/Salary	Other	Total
Mar.	73	707	435	55	1,424
Apr.	310	213	151	114	788
May	479	76	185	73	813
June	421	115	155	165	856
July	261	140	149	298	848
Aug.	528	193	171	113	1,005
Sept.	493	364	101	193	1,151
Oct.	1,002	462	167	218	1,849
Nov.	676	314	122	251	1,363
Dec.	1,395	192	308	302	2,197
Jan.	615	280	216	288	1,399
Feb.	222	398	53	242	915
Total annual income	6,329	3,454	2,213	2,312	14,308

Source: Chalamwong and Meyer (1982).

Table 6.4   Employed Thai Population by Occupation, 1986 (percent)

Occupation	Female	Male	Total
Farming, fishing, hunting	30.0	36.0	66.0
Sales	5.6	3.9	9.5
Crafts, manual laborers	4.3	7.2	11.5
Services	1.7	1.6	3.3
Professional, technical	1.5	1.8	3.3
Clerical	1.2	1.3	2.5
Administrative and managerial	0.3	1.1	1.4

Source: Labour Force Survey (May 1986).

Table 6.5   Average Monthly Thai Wages (Bt), 1986

Area and Sex	Private Employee	Public Employee
Female		
Municipal	1,997.5	4,086.2
Non-municipal	1,168.5	3,265.0
Male		
Municipal	2,999.1	4,588.5
Non-municipal	1,650.5	2,957.5

Source: Labour Force Survey (February 1986).

References

Introduction

Banerjee, Nirmala. "Outline of Paper on Conceptual and Methodological Issues Related to Integration of Women's Concerns in Development Planning." Prepared for the Expert Group Meeting on the Integration of Women's Concerns in Development Planning, ESCAP, Bangkok, June 5–7, 1989.

Bardhan, Kalpana. "Women's Work and Lives in Some South and Southeast Asian Countries: In Relation to Family Strategies in Various Macro Contexts." Paper prepared as part of the United Nations University project, Comparative Study of Women's Work and Family Strategies in South and Southeast Asia, September 1987, mimeo.

Bruce, Judith, and Daisy Dwyer, "Introduction." In *A Home Divided: Women and Income in the Third World,* ed. Daisy Dwyer and Judith Bruce. Stanford, Calif.: Stanford University Press, 1988.

Corner, Lorraine. "Human Resources Development for Developing Countries: A Survey of the Major Theoretical Issues." In *Human Resources Development in Asia and the Pacific: Its Social Dimension.* Bangkok: ESCAP, 1986.

Economic and Social Commission for Asia and the Pacific (ESCAP). "Regional Development Strategy for the 1980s." Bangkok, 1979, mimeo.

———. *Achievements of the United Nations Decade for Women in Asia and the Pacific.* Bangkok: ESCAP, 1987.

———. *Asia-Pacific in Figures 1989.* Bangkok: ESCAP, 1989.

INSTRAW (United Nations International Research and Training Institute for the Advancement of Women), n.d. Quoted in United Nations Nongovernmental Liaison Service, *Women and World Economic Crisis,* Women and Development Kit No. 6, Geneva.

Jain, Devaki, and Nirmala Banerjee, eds. *The Tyranny of the Household:*

Investigative Essays on Women's Work. New Delhi: Shakti Books, 1985.
Krishna, Raj. *Women and Development Planning* (with special reference to Asia and the Pacific). Kuala Lumpur: Asian and Pacific Development Center, 1983.
Kumar, Shubh. "Composition of Economic Constraints in Child Nutrition: Impact from Maternal Incomes and Employment in Low-Income Households." Ph.D. dissertation. Cornell University, 1977.
Overholt, Catherine A., Mary B. Anderson, Kathleen Cloud, and James E. Austin. *Gender Roles in Development Projects.* West Hartford, Conn.: Kumarian Press, 1985.
Population Crisis Committee. "Country Rankings of the Status of Women: Poor, Powerless and Pregnant." Population Briefing Paper No. 20, June 1988.
Rao, Arunashree P. "Incorporating Gender Issues in Development Training." Bangkok, Population Council, 1986.
Sen, Amartya K. *Gender and Cooperative Conflicts.* WIDER Working Paper No. 18, Helsinki, July 1987.
―――. "The Relative Deprivation of Women." Speech delivered at the ESCAP Expert Group Meeting on Integrating Women's Concerns in Development Planning, Bangkok, June 5, 1989.
Tendler, Judith. "What Ever Happened to Poverty Alleviation?" Report prepared for the Ford Foundation, March 1987, mimeo.
Tonguthai, Pawadee. "Women and Work in Thailand and the Philippines." In *Women's Economic Participation in Asia and the Pacific.* Bangkok: ESCAP, 1987.

Gender Analysis Framework

Boserup, Ester. *Women's Role in Economic Development.* London: George Allen and Unwin Ltd., 1970.
Huntington, Sue Ellen. "Issues in Women's Role in Economic Development: Critique and Alternatives." *Journal of Marriage and the Family* 37, no. 4 (November 1975): 1001–1012.
Korten, David C. "Community Organization and Rural Development: A Learning Process Approach." *Public Administration Review* 40 (1980), pp. 480–503.
Rogers, Barbara. *The Domestication of Women: Discrimination in Developing Societies.* London: Tavistock Publications, 1980.
Scott, Gloria. *The Invisible Woman.* Washington, D.C.: World Bank, 1980.

Case 1

Chowdhury, P. K., M. R. Karim, and S. Begum. "Chandpur Irrigation Project: Socio-Economic Impact on Different Classes of Households and Genders." Unpublished manuscript, Bangladesh Academy for Rural

Development, Comilla, 1989.

Islam, Mahmuda. "Impact of Large-Scale Development Projects on Women: A Study of Four Villages." Unpublished manuscript, 1988.

Thompson, Paul M. "Bangladesh's Chandpur Irrigation Project: The Fortunes of a Major Water Management Scheme." Working paper, Flood Hazard Research Center, Middlesex Polytechnic, Queensway, 1986.

Case 2

Rao, Arunashree P. "The Impact of Qualitative Improvements in Education on Retention at the Primary Level in India: A Review of the Literature and Recent Empirical Evidence." Indian Institute of Management, Ahmedabad, March 1985.

————. "The School Incentives Program: A Case Study of the Ambakach Primary School, Limkheda Taluka, Gujarat." Indian Institute of Management, Ahmedabad, April 1985.

Case 3

Acharya, Sarthi, and V. G. Panwalkar. "The Maharashtra Employment Guarantee Scheme: Impacts on Male and Female Labor," Arunashree P. Rao and Randee Falk, eds. Population Council, Bangkok, March 1988.

Gupta, Anil K., with Y. Mandavkar, S. Amin, and R. Shah. "Role of Women in Risk Adjustment in Drought-Prone Regions." Working Paper No. 704, Indian Institute of Management, Ahmedabad, India, October 1987.

Case 4

Joseph, Rebecca. *Worker, Middlewomen, Entrepreneur: Women in the Indonesian Batik Industry.* Population Council, Regional Office for South and East Asia, Bangkok, 1987. Available through Kumarian Press.

Case 5

Donzina, G., Jr., and A. C. Early. "Benchmark Report on the Socioeconomic Conditions of the NIA-Ford Assisted Communal Irrigation Systems in Camarines Sur." Paper presented to the San Jose–Magadap Humanitarian Irrigators' Association (SJMHIA) and the San Isidro, Bahay, Aslong, and Palangon (SIBAP) Irrigators' Association, April 26, 1981.

Illo, Jeanne Frances I. "Wives at Work: Patterns of Labor Force Participation in Two Rice-Farming Villages in the Philippines." In IRRI, *Women in Rice Farming.* Aldershot, England: Gower Publishing, 1985.

————. "Irrigation in the Philippines: Impact on Women and Their Households—The Aslong Project Case." Population Council, Bangkok, May 1988.

Illo, Jeanne Frances I., Romana P. de los Reyes, and Nestor S. Felix. *Organizing Farmers for Communal Irrigation: Preconstruction and Construction in the Aslong Irrigation Project.* Quezon City: Institute of Philippine Culture, Ateneo de Manila University, 1984.

Illo, Jeanne Frances I., and Jesus R. Volante. *Organizing Farmers for Communal Irrigation: Operation and Maintenance in the Aslong and Taisan Irrigation Systems.* Naga City: Research and Service Center, Ateneo de Naga, 1984.

Case 6

Chalamwong, Yonguth, and Richard I. Meyer. *Farm Household Income Levels, Sources and Patterns in Selected Thai Villages.* Kasetsart University, Bangkok, Thailand, 1982.

Labour Force Survey, September 1983, February 1986 and May 1986. National Statistical Office, published in *Information about Labour and Women,* Thailand Development Research Institute Foundation, n.d.

Meyer, R. L., et al. "Agricultural Credit in Thailand." Department of Agricultural Economics and Rural Sociology, Ohio State University, Columbus, Ohio, for USAID, Thailand, May 1979.

Palmer, Ingrid, et al. "The Northeast Rainfed Agricultural Development Project in Thailand: A Baseline Survey of Women's Roles and Household Resource Allocation for a Farming Systems Approach." In *Case Studies of the Impact of Large-scale Development Projects on Women: A Series for Planners.* Population Council, New York, September 1983.

Rao, Aruna. "The Muek-Lek Women's Dairy Project in Thailand." SEEDS Series. New York: SEEDS, 1990.

Royal Thai Government, 1986. National Economic and Social Development Board, Bangkok.

TEAM Consulting Engineers Co., Ltd. with EMPIRE Consulting Engineers Co., Ltd. "Land Reform Areas Project: Final Report, Saraburi, Sub-Project Proposal." Ministry of Agriculture and Cooperatives, Agricultural Land Reform Office, Thailand, August 1986.

Thomson, Suteera. "A Concept Paper: The Role of Thai Women in Development." Thailand Development Research Institute Foundation, Bangkok, April 22, 1988.

About the Editors

ARUNA RAO has for five years coordinated the Population Council program on Women's Roles and Gender Differences in Development, under whose auspices most of the cases in this volume were prepared. On behalf of the program, she has worked closely with researchers in developing new frameworks for gender analysis, with project planners and managers in working through the policy and management implications of gender issues, and with donors and other international agency personnel in building support for incorporating the findings of the study into ongoing development planning. She holds a doctorate in educational administration from Columbia University and currently lives in Dhaka, Bangladesh.

MARY B. ANDERSON is President of the Collaborative for Development Action, a small consulting firm based in Cambridge, Massachusetts. She holds a doctorate in development economics from the University of Colorado in Boulder and has consulted with and carried out training for many international and bilateral development agencies. Her major fields of work include gender analysis and case method training, access to education, and the relationships between disasters and development. Her field work has been primarily in Asia and eastern Africa.

CATHERINE A. OVERHOLT is Vice President of the Collaborative for Development Action. She holds a doctorate in health economics from the Harvard School of Public Health and she has consulted with and conducted training for many multilateral and bilateral development agencies. Her major fields of work include gender issues, health economics and financing public health systems, case writing and case method training. Her field work has been primarily in Latin America and Africa.

Catherine Overholt and Mary Anderson are part of the original team that developed the Gender Analysis Framework and case training approach in cooperation with USAID's Office of Women in Development and the Harvard Institute for International Development. They were co-editors, with Kathleen Cloud and James E. Austin, of the groundbreaking *Gender Roles in Development Projects: A Case Book*, published by Kumarian Press in 1985.